TO GET RICH IS GLORIOUS

Pantheon Books ★ New York

To
Get
Rich
Is
Glorious

CHINA IN THE EIGHTIES

Orville
Schell

Published in the United States
by Pantheon Books,
a division of Random House, Inc., New York,
and simultaneously in Canada
by Random House of Canada Limited,
Toronto.
Most of this work originally appeared in
The New Yorker.
Library of Congress Cataloging in Publication Data
Schell, Orville.
To get rich is glorious.
1. China—Description and travel—1976–
2. Schell, Orville.
I. Title.
DS712.S33 1985   951.05′8   84–42697
ISBN 0-394-53952-4
Manufactured in the United States of America
First Edition
Book design: Elissa Ichiyasu

For my son

Ole

with love,

and

in anticipation

of that time

when we can go

to China

together

Acknowledgments

With thanks, as ever, to my editor at Pantheon, Tom Engelhardt, for the enormous amount of time and energy, as well as unique talent, that he lavishes on the books he publishes, and to Sara Lippincott, my editor at *The New Yorker*, whose editorial insight and thoroughness were so important in bringing out the best in these pieces. To Elizabeth Tuomi, a note of gratitude for her intelligence and good cheer in correcting and typing the final manuscripts. And many thanks to John Service for his careful scrutiny of the manuscript.

Orville Schell

September, 1984
Bolinas, California

Note:

One Chinese yuan (¥) is roughly equal in value to $.50 U.S.

The Wind of Wanting to Go It Alone

PART ONE

For anyone familiar with the great cities of Asia, which teem with activity, it was eerie to walk the streets of urban China while Mao stilled lived. In Chairman Mao's China, all private enterprises, even individual street venders, had been branded "tails of capitalism." And so diligently had the government gone about chopping off these tails that the streets looked as if a neutron-bomb-like device had been detonated, destroying small businesses while leaving everything else intact. There were no curbside restaurants with their smells of food wafting in the air, no peddlers hawking their wares, no throngs of shoppers browsing and haggling with merchants on the sidewalks. The streets of Mao's China were crowded, but with silent, purposeful people, buying the bare necessities of life from dreary state-owned stores or going to and from work.

When I first went to China, in 1975, Mao Zedong and the so-called Gang of Four, led by Mao's wife, Jiang Qing, were still firmly in power. The shadow of the Chinese Communist Party fell across all aspects of life, freezing the Chinese people in a combination of fear and socialist rectitude. Politics was "in command." To put one's own interests above those of the Party and the task of "building socialism" was a dangerous form of heresy. And to be branded a heretic in a land where there were few places to hide and fewer ways to escape was a grim prospect indeed. Should one momentarily forget the Party's dedication to creating a "new socialist man," who would, in Mao's words, "serve the people" with all his "heart and soul," slogans were everywhere—on billboards, walls, smokestacks, ships, dams, buildings, even mountainsides—as reminders:

NEVER FORGET CLASS STRUGGLE

CARRY THE REVOLUTION THROUGH TO THE END

DOWN WITH ALL CAPITALIST ROADERS

Travelling in China at that time, I felt as if I had fallen down a well, like Alice into Wonderland, and entered a strange new universe in which all the imperatives of the outside world had been reversed. Whereas other countries eagerly sought to build economic relations with their neighbors, China was dedicated to isolation and self-reliance. Whereas most governments accepted class divisions, China's leaders waged an unceasing battle against them. And while most governments viewed politics as simply one aspect of life, China's leaders viewed it as life itself.

I returned to China several times after Mao's death, in 1976, and I watched as the country cautiously began a cultural transformation. Like a piece of paper in a fire, whose edges slowly burn before the flames finally move inward to incinerate the center, old-style Chinese Communism was beginning to be consumed by change. Western influences were penetrating China's protective isolationism, creating unlikely contrasts. The Chinese people, once so mute, were beginning to express their curiosity about the outside world. Politics slowly receded in importance as China's leadership implemented a new political "line" stressing a pragmatic approach to rebuilding the country's economy rather than class struggle.

A new political line is the Chinese Communist equivalent of the Christian notion of being born again. It offers the opportunity to jettison a bungled past and sally forth on a different political course into a better future. This is exactly how Mao Zedong came to power years ago, when the Chinese Revolution was rising from the ashes of traditional China. He and other leftist intellectuals struggled to detach China from its Confucian past and to regroup the Chinese people behind a new ideology and identity, derived from the teachings of Marx and Lenin.

Now the Chinese Communist Party has declared Mao's political line defunct. Under the leadership of Deng Xiaoping, who consolidated his power in a series of political maneuvers in the late nineteen-seventies, China's doors have been thrown open to the outside world. Militant egalitarianism and class politics have been abandoned in favor of production. "Black cat, white cat—it's a good cat if it catches mice," Deng has told his people.

The first stirrings of change became evident in 1979 and 1980. Democracy Wall, on which Peking's activists posted petitions demanding greater freedom, came and went. So-called free markets, where peasants were allowed to sell produce from their recently reinstated private plots, began to appear all over China. The notion of working for one's own benefit rather than for the abstraction of socialism began to be discussed. Incomes started to rise. After 1981, these forces gathered full momentum, and when I first arrived back in Peking, in July of 1983, after an absence of less than two years, I found the streets markedly transformed. I felt as if I were walking back in on a film that had mysteriously speeded up in my absence, so that by the time I regained my seat a whole new plot development had begun; it was hard to imagine how, short of being at war, a country could begin to change so fast.

The Chinese Communist Party has always been fond of using the term *da gao*, which means "to do something in a big way"—as in "to build socialism in a big way" or "to start a mass movement in a big way." Although the present leaders of China, unlike their predecessors, now view political mass movements as disruptive and unproductive, they have lost none of the old penchant for doing things in a big way. Their current project is the decentralization and decollectivization of the Chinese economy—a radical departure from the past, which they have embraced with an almost desperate optimism and exhilaration.

★

As I set out my first morning in Peking to walk through the outdoor market that had sprung up on Dongsixi Street, in the quarter known as the East City, the first signs of change I encountered were several "tails of capitalism." An old woman squatting on the sidewalk was selling an ecumenical collection of gilt plaster statues of Buddha and the Virgin Mary. Next to her stood a young man with a tray slung around his neck; he was selling snapshots of singers and movie stars, many of whom lived in Taiwan or Hong Kong. A little farther down the street, I saw a man with a tall bamboo pole strapped to his back. Dangling from the pole on a string was a life-size cardboard cutout of a sewing machine, which had a needle affixed to it. Drawing closer, I saw that the man held a small aluminum device shaped like a fighter-bomber, with which he threaded the needle over and over with masterly ease. "Just amazing, I tell you!" he was saying in a throaty, rapid-fire rap like that of a Forty-second Street cardsharp. "There's nothing like it on the market. It saves time! Cannot be purchased at a store! Would you like one, or two?" At this point in his pitch, he paused and, holding the aluminum gizmo up in the air, gazed in turn at several women in the onlooking throng. Sales were brisk. Next in line on the sidewalk was an old man who sat patiently and silently on a tiny wooden stool before a motley offering of medicinal bones, roots, and herbs spread out on a back issue of the *Worker's Daily*. Nearby, a severe-looking middle-aged woman sold a Chinese version of typists' white-out. As a knot of curious people gathered around her, she bent over a pad of paper and inscribed a Chinese character with a traditional writing brush and ink. Then, taking some liquid from a large brown bottle, she swabbed the paper, making the black character vanish in an instant.

On a short street that runs toward the People's Market, the sidewalks were chockablock with small booths, all displaying retailers' licenses on cloth banners—a formality most of the more itinerant peddlers ignored. These booths were constructed of boards laid across sawhorses, or were simply set up on the backs of the bicycle carts in which the goods were hauled to and from the makeshift market each day. An elaborate patchwork of plastic tarpaulins was stretched overhead to keep out the scorching sun and the occasional shower. Most of these merchants sold clothing, with a heavy emphasis on T-shirts—an item of apparel that young Chinese are particularly fond of these days. T-shirts made in Hong Kong or abroad confer the most status on a wearer. One youth I spotted in Beihai Park—formerly a preserve of the Imperial family—wore a T-shirt inscribed with the message "Uncle Sam's Misguided Children, Beijing, China." A Chinese construction worker who was working on the remodelling of the International Club wore a T-shirt marked "Department of Commerce, Narcotics Squad." Perhaps the most popular T-shirt—so popular, in fact, that I could not find one anywhere in Peking to buy for myself— showed a picture of a bodybuilder's naked body. Beneath one flexed arm were written the words "Vigorous and Graceful."

In fact, in June of 1982 *China Youth News* had run an article declaring that young Chinese who wore T-shirts imprinted with such English-language messages as "Kiss Me" or "U.S.A." were guilty of "ignorance, exhibitionism, and spiritual pollution." The Communist Youth League paper denounced Chinese shops that printed and sold such shirts, saying that they were only "catering to some people's blind worship of foreign things and a base taste for profit." However, few youths seemed deterred from wearing such T-shirts by these admonitions.

As I neared the corner, two dissolute-looking youths wearing dark glasses arrived with a bicycle cart and began setting up shop beside the curb. They were selling what looked like men's shirts in bright-colored plaids. Since men in China do not ordinarily wear bright colors, such as red—these are reserved for women and children—I walked over to the cart for a closer inspection. Unlike the other venders, these two young men displayed no license. When I examined the label on one of their shirts, I saw the name Sears, and when I asked them who their supplier was, they just looked at each other with sly smiles and laughed.

At the end of T-shirt alley, I spotted a pedicab, its driver dozing on the passenger seat while he awaited a fare. I was surprised to see a pedicab; these small, rickshaw-like conveyances, which are powered by a man on a bicycle rather than on foot, had long been banned in China. The image of one human being straining on a bicycle to haul another human being around was one that came too close to suggesting the old exploitative society the Communists had set out to transform with their revolution. But sensitivity to such socialist niceties is evidently on the wane, for as I watched, a potato-shaped woman, carrying several net bags bulging with food and packages, rudely tapped the driver on the chest with her fan and woke him up. After haggling over the price, she heaved her bulk into the pedicab and barked an order, and a moment later they were off, the calf muscles of the driver flexing as he struggled to get his vehicle moving. It was the first time I had seen such a sight since the early seventies, when pedicabs were replaced by taxis on Taiwan.

After a long absence, a private sector is rapidly reappearing in China's economy, and a new class of privately employed Chinese is beginning to appear along with it. In October of 1981, Party and government leaders gave their official blessing to the proliferation of private businesses. In the first six months of 1983, retail sales by state-owned commercial enterprises were 2.5 per cent higher than they had been in the same period in 1981, whereas sales by private businesses that had bothered to get government licenses were 110 per cent higher. There are now privately run repair shops for television sets and radios, bicycles and motorcycles. Private barbers and shoemakers work in almost every neighborhood, and myriad peddlers and repairmen, with their distinctive cries, have once again begun to roam the city's back alleys. Night markets have begun to spring up in busy sections of Peking, such as Wangfujing and Xuanwu, for the first time in years. Outdoor film processors have set up shop. Private tailors, the fashion among those who can afford them have proliferated, and become so deluged with work, that by 1984 many customers found themselves waiting two or three months to get a suit or dress made.

Cooks, maids, and nannies—once considered bourgeois affectations—are becoming commonplace in the households of middle-income families as well as in those of wealthy professionals. In fact, in February of 1984 the *Economic Daily*, a Shanghai-published newspaper covering finance, printed an article by Yang Zhengyan, the deputy general secretary of the Peking municipal government, extolling the establishment of the newly founded Housework Service Company, the capital's first privately run agency dedicated to finding jobs for domestics. In his article, "The Question of Housekeepers and the Socialization of Housework," Yang noted: "Although the employment of household help was criticized as gentrified, bourgeois, and exploitative during the Cultural Revolution, in reality such employment cannot be abolished."

Why not?

"The current tendency is for people to want to have less housework and more time for work, study, and recreation," Yang explained, concluding that for those who could afford them, maids in China were now "an inevitable phenomenon of today's urban social life."

In March of 1984, the *Beijing Daily* reported that the Housework Service Company already had 2,500 customers and was getting "loud applause" from city residents, who were said to be already employing more than 30,000 live-in maids, many of them imported from poor rural areas. Down south in Canton, the Guangdong Labor Service Company announced an even bolder plan. In July, having gained approval in concept from the Chinese government, it applied for permission from Hong Kong immigration authorities to "export" cooks and cleaning women to the colony, where five hundred families had already contracted to hire them.

Entrepreneurs were starting to open up small private inns, which Chinese travellers now often prefer, because these establishments are cheaper than the state-run hotels and sometimes offer meals at no extra charge. When the government began encouraging this practice as part of the responsibility system, there was an explosion of these inns, some several stories high and offering color TVs, carpeting, and private bathrooms. For instance, by the spring of 1984, the New China News Agency was reporting that more than 158 private inns had sprung up around scenic Mount Emei, a famous tourist destination in Sichuan province. A friend told me that, in an effort to get customers, some of these private inns now even include a young woman in the price of a night's lodging.

One particularly lucrative form of private enterprise is the restaurant business. Part of the reason a private restaurant can be so successful is that state-owned Chinese restaurants are among the most depressing places in the world. Although the food is not necessarily bad and prices are reasonable (particularly by Western standards), the restaurants themselves are almost invariably noisy, dirty, ill-lit, crowded, ugly, and badly managed. At mealtimes, one has to wait in line to get in the door, and once inside, one must usually eat at a table heaped with the debris of earlier dinners. Employees are often lackadaisical, even surly and discourteous, and are more concerned with getting the customers out the door so the establishment can close promptly at 7 P.M. than with providing good service. (A few years ago, I was invited to a private banquet at the Sichuan Restaurant, one of Peking's best, by a friend who is a high-ranking official. Halfway through our dinner, the waitresses began turning off the fans and lights to signal us that it was nearly closing time.)

Interested in seeing what dining in China is like at one of the new private restaurants, I went out one night with two friends to the Jinjin Restaurant, at the corner of Di'anmennei and Di'anmenxi streets, behind the Imperial City. The Jinjin was surprisingly spacious—unlike most private restaurants, which are crammed into tiny rooms. In Peking, where overcrowding is legendary and living or working space is at a premium, a location like the Jinjin's, facing on a main street, can usually be obtained only if the proprietor has *guanxi*, or "special relations," with an influential official or with someone who works in the municipal office responsible for assigning commercial space.

The Jinjin Restaurant was run by a family: the daughter cooked, the mother waited on table, and the father sat with his abacus behind the front counter, handling the accounts. By Chinese standards, the restaurant was handsomely appointed. Fluorescent fixtures cast a brilliant light. Fans churned the hot summer air, making it possible to eat without sweating. The walls were adorned with examples of Chinese calligraphy. There were six tables, each covered with a plastic sheet and uncluttered by the usual assortment of fish heads, gristle, and bones. The food, which was at least twice as expensive as that in the state-owned restaurants, was as delicious as any I have eaten in China. It was served courteously by the harried mother, who scurried back and forth between the kitchen and the tables. A Chinese-made Snowflake refrigerator near the front counter valiantly battled the heat to produce partly cooled bottles of Peking beer. As we dined, I realized that this was one of the few times on all my trips to China when I was actually enjoying a meal that was not served in a fancy tourist restaurant or in one of the special back rooms that many of the better state-owned restaurants maintain for "foreign guests" and other dignitaries.

But the Jinjin is, in its own way, a preserve of privilege. It is one of the growing number of refuges from the madding crowd which the new Chinese system allows its own people to enjoy—if they can afford to. After years of militantly thwarting any individuals who found a way to surge ahead of the pack economically, the Chinese leadership has now accepted the fact that not all people are or will be equal and has in fact even begun leasing many state-owned restaurants to private managers, many of whom quite promptly get rich. It has decided that as long as the productive forces of the nation are generally moving forward, growing discrepancies between rich and poor, and even the development of an incipient bourgeoisie, are an acceptable price to pay. Mao Zedong, of course, advocated an ideal of classless, equal development, in which no individual or segment of society was to advance at the expense of another. The salaries of educated people were not to rise faster than those of common workers. City people were not to enjoy more improvements in their standard of living than peasants in the countryside. In short, it was considered politically incorrect for any individual or family to become wealthy while others remained poor. Mao thought of himself as the great leveller.

In December of 1978, two years after Mao's death, the Third Plenum of the Eleventh Party Central Committee convened in Peking. The session declared that turbulent mass struggles were no longer the order of the day, and that if China was to develop successfully, it must turn from class struggle to "modernization" and completely restructure its economy. After a decade of the Cultural Revolution, with "politics in command," the Chinese people were told to "seek truth from facts" rather than from political ideology. They were told that their ability to produce, rather than their "socialist purity," would be the new measure of success. The Central Committee called for the abandonment of the old Stalinist model of production, which rigidly maintained all planning and decision-making authority in the hands of the central ministries. Over the next few years, much of this authority began to be dispersed downward, so that state-owned businesses became more independent economic units and their managers became responsible in large measure for planning, use of capital, distribution of profits —in short, for their success or failure. Workers had for years received a flat salary of between thirty and fifty-five yuan a month (two yuan are approximately equivalent to one United States dollar) no matter how efficiently they produced; now many of them found their pay geared to their output, with bonuses promised if business was good.

From the Third Plenum onward, a new concept of industrial management and a new work ethic began to spread outward from Peking. Workers who had been terrified of evincing even the slightest bourgeois taint were told that it was all right to serve themselves as well as "the people." GET RICH BY WORKING ran one slogan. TO GET RICH IS GLORIOUS proclaimed another. Deng Xiaoping, in his *Selected*

Works, published in July of 1983, wrote that it was now ideologically correct "to make some people rich first, so as to lead all the people to wealth."

They were arresting slogans for a Communist Party that had formerly threatened anyone who exhibited any privatistic tendencies or interest in personal gain with the ignominy of being labelled a "capitalist roader," a "rightist," or—the last degree of political damnation—a "counter-revolutionary." In the past, people may have entertained fantasies of wealth, but few dared express them. Like fame, bourgeois contamination made one stand out; as an old Chinese aphorism put it, "People are just as afraid of becoming well known as a pig is of becoming fat." Party theoreticians now undertook not only to justify economic inequality but actually to speak of a need to "overcome egalitarianism," as if egalitarianism were an insidious force completely at odds with the Chinese Revolution. One particularly striking bit of evidence that China's era of egalitarianism has ended was the announcement in 1983 by the People's Liberation Army that badges of rank, which had been abolished in 1965 by former Defense Minister Lin Biao, would be restored in August, 1984.

Many Chinese, particularly intellectuals, were relieved at the turn of events; still, they were wary. In China, political lines come and go quickly and without warning or explanation. Even now, five years after the reforms were begun, many Chinese felt uneasy about publicly displaying private wealth or being visibly committed to one extreme in a political world that has always had the potential to snap back with an equal and opposite reaction.

An expatriate American friend who has worked at the Foreign Languages Press, in Peking, for many years told me a story she had heard which expresses the ambiguity many Chinese felt about publicly displaying private wealth: "The leaders of one village called a meeting at which they specifically requested attendance by all families that made over five thousand yuan in the past year. Even though there was a well-publicized official campaign in China to celebrate what the Party has dubbed 'ten-thousand-yuan households'—households earning more than ten thousand yuan a year, or about thirty times the national average—several families in the village who had made five thousand yuan failed to show up, because they were afraid they might be publicly criticized as 'capitalist roaders.' The next day, they learned that the meeting had been called to honor them as 'model households,' not to chastise them."

To allay such fears, the Party launched a propaganda campaign to reassure those who still suspected that the new economic reforms were a passing fancy. In June of 1983, a self-employed photographer, a private chicken farmer who had earned 20,000 yuan in one year, and another privately employed man, described as a "bartender," became members of the prestigious National People's Congress, the rubber-stamp legislative organ of the Chinese government. The selection of such people under Mao and the Gang of Four would have been roughly equivalent to the seating of an avowed Marxist revolutionary in the United States Senate. In August, the government organized a conference in Peking which brought together more than three hundred delegates from all across China who had been successful in setting up individual or collective private enterprises. They were addressed by none other than Party General Secretary Hu Yaobang. Sounding like the president of a local chamber of commerce, he asked these latter-day model workers, "What would our markets and lives be like if there were no collective and individual economies to serve the daily needs of the people? . . . Every job that benefits the country and the people is to be respected." Hu went on to criticize people who still held the "outdated" view that workers in state-owned enterprises were more "ideologically respectable" than those in private business.

Soon after, newspaper articles expressing approval of wealth gained through "hard work" began to appear everywhere. Some bore headlines that could almost have been lifted directly from the newspapers of Taiwan or Hong Kong. HAVE NO FEAR OF BECOMING PROSPEROUS proclaimed one. MORE INDIVIDUAL ENTERPRISES NOW, BUT NOT ENOUGH and PROTECT INITIATIVE OF PEASANTS WHO BECOME WELL OFF advised others.

From the looks of things, this propaganda offensive had already proved highly successful. More and more people seemed to be making more and more money with greater and greater vigor. In the English-language *China Daily*, one rich peasant from Hebei province analyzed his situation this way: "In 1982 I became prosperous on the sly. In 1983 I had to be brave to remain prosperous. In 1984 I can be prosperous without any worry." One index of this prosperity was the boom in advertising. By the spring of 1984, China's 2,340 advertising units—in 1979 there were only 10—were doing 2.5 million yuan of business annually. The country's 305 newspapers, 633 magazines, 115 radio stations, and 57 TV stations had started running advertisements.

Many Chinese now had television sets, and political battles were being fought out on television, for the first time in Chinese history. One night, in the one-room apartment of some Chinese friends, I watched a documentary about a man named Rong Yiren, a Shanghai millionaire whose family had made its fortune in textiles and flour before the Revolution. When China was "liberated," in 1949, Rong remained in Shanghai, presided over the nationalization of his family's factories, and in 1959 became viceminister of the textile industry. However, in the political storms that swept back and forth across China in the following years, Rong was defamed and lost his official standing. After the fall of the Gang of Four, in 1977, the "verdict was reversed" on Rong. He was rehabilitated as a "national capitalist"—meaning that even though he had a capitalist background, he was considered a patriot—and he was thus deemed fit to serve his country again. In 1979, he was appointed chairman of the board of the newly formed

China International Trust and Investment Corporation, which has a mandate from the Chinese government to seek out foreign capital for investment in China.

The film opened in Rong's palatial house, which was fiilled with relatives. As the camera panned around his extended family, Rong hovered benevolently, in the manner of a mandarin patriarch, making polite conversation. There was, however, nothing of the traditional mandarin about Rong's appearance—he was casually dressed, in Western clothes, and looked extremely debonair. Another sequence showed him watching reruns of a soccer game on a videotape recorder; in yet another, he sat in a meditative pose, eyes serenely closed, listening to a recording of Beethoven's "Moonlight" Sonata. Then the camera cut to a portrayal of the other side of Rong—the Chinese side—and he was shown gazing admiringly at a wall hanging by the renowned Chinese painter Qi Baishi. The closing scene was filmed inside Rong's Mercedes-Benz limousine, the camera peering through the windshield out over the hood ornament, as he headed off to work, presumably to serve his country patriotically by rubbing elbows with Western capitalists. The documentary was narrated by a male announcer, in the high-pitched and urgent voice (imagine a blend of sportscasting and Peking Opera) reserved for broadcasts about ranking leaders.

When the short film ended, I turned to my two friends—who had been watching mainly out of deference to my interest—and asked them what they thought its significance was.

"The idea is that class struggle is over and it is all right to be wealthy again," said one, a graduate student at Peking University, with a cryptic smile on his face.

My other friend, who works in a state-owned business in the city, said scornfully, "First, the Party spends thirty years tearing down the bourgeoisie because they are supposedly hindering the Chinese Revolution. Now it's going to spend thirty years building them back up to help carry out the Chinese Revolution. The message is that you can now love your country by getting rich."

The night I ate at the Jinjin Restaurant, I noticed two young men wolfing down plates of food and bottles of beer on the other side of the room. They were not to be confused with the likes of Rong Yiren, but the splendor of their meal suggested that they might at least be among China's *nouveaux riches*. They both sported mustaches and wore a curious ensemble of clothes: dusty plastic sandals, equally inelegant sleeveless undershirts, and matching pairs of cream-colored, pleated sharkskin trousers that looked as if they had come out of the wardrobe of F. Scott Fitzgerald. The two sat quietly, eying the rest of the room with studied coolness, chain-smoking cigarettes, eating three or four dishes of food, and drinking beer until their faces glowed like jack-o'-lanterns. Their meal must have cost ten or twelve yuan—roughly a fifth of the average factory worker's monthly salary. After dinner, I looked over and caught the eye of one of the youths. Cocking his head, he grinned drowsily, and called out, "Hey, foreign friend! Let's have some beer together."

These young men were what Chinese refer to as *liumang* —a word that has no satisfactory equivalent in English. Chinese dictionaries translate *liumang* as "hooligan" or "hoodlum," but that gives only a partial suggestion of its meaning. Most *liumang* are youths who are unemployed— or what the Chinese somewhat euphemistically refer to as *daiye* ("waiting for employment"). Although the Chinese government once proudly proclaimed the superiority of the socialist over the capitalist system on the ground that unemployment was "impossible" (the government could always force factories to hire more people, even if they weren't needed, since the factories were state-owned), it now admits that it has a problem. In some cities, unemployment in 1982 was running as high as 12 per cent, and one of the main rationalizations for private enterprise in

China today is that it provides jobs. (By the middle of 1984, the Chinese were claiming that their new economic policies had cut unemployment by 60 per cent.) But in truth the unemployed have to make their own jobs, and most *liumang* prefer to do this by hustling and scrambling on the margins of organized Chinese life, some of them turning to out-and-out crime.

I walked over to the table, and as I sat down, Liumang No. 1 clamped a cigarette between his teeth and poured me some beer. After a few amenities, I asked them how they could afford such an expensive dinner.

"We get things for people," replied Liumang No. 2, his speech slightly slurred by the effect of the beer.

"We can get you anything you want," added Liumang No. 1 jauntily.

"What kinds of things?"

"Anything you want," repeated No. 1. "Clothes from Hong Kong, tape recorders, cameras, watches, televisions, radios."

"We can even get you women," said No. 2, leaning forward and lowering his voice to a conspiratorial whisper.

"Could you get fifty bottles of Qingdao beer?" I asked.

"Hey! No problem," replied Liumang No. 1, blowing a cloud of cigarette smoke out over my head. "When do you want them?"

"What does it take?" I asked.

"Money. Cold cash—that's the only thing that counts these days," Liumang No. 2 said, smiling and reaching out with his chopsticks to snag a roast peanut from a dish of hors d'oeuvres.

Although some *liumang* engage in serious crime, much of their "hooliganism" involves dressing in Western fashions calculated to outrage their conservative elders, indulging in libertine sexual behavior whenever possible, and occasionally engaging in petty theft. Generally, the mainstay of their existence is the buying and selling of goods through what the Chinese refer to as "the back door." Many of the goods sold by private retailers on the street come through the back door: that is, they were originally manufactured in a state-owned factory for sale in a state-owned store. Somewhere along the line, these goods are siphoned off into the private sector by a person in a responsible position in return for a bribe or a favor.

The *liumang* are actually only one species in a whole new genus of people engaged in *touji daoba*, or "speculation and profiteering," centering on the sale of goods that are often illegally acquired. Such activities have spawned a new vocabulary in Chinese business. *Erdao fenzi*, for instance, are small-time urban entrepreneurs who will buy and resell almost anything if there is enough profit in it. The *paodan-bang*, or "running gangs of one," are another category of speculators, who deal principally in luxury items, many of which are smuggled into China from abroad, and often transport them great distances to make a profit. Profiteers are playing a larger and larger role in the distribution of everything from food and clothes to the most specialized consumer goods. They are also causing some problems. An example is the shortage of beer in state-run outlets during the hot summer months, when the supply from breweries can't keep up with the demand. So much beer is sold through the back door to private restaurants and the like that normal people find it almost impossible to buy any from state-run stores. Instead, they must either do without or pay inflated prices to private sellers.

The Chinese government is, of course, concerned about this phenomenon; the resale of back-door goods by private individuals at premium prices fuels inflation without contributing anything to producton. The State Council, the administrative branch of the central government, has endeavored to control such profiteering by issuing regulations that strictly forbid it. But, if anything, the practice has grown more widespread recently. With so many shady elements like the *liumang*, the *erdao fenzi*, and the *paodanbang* wheeling and dealing, and with the number of legitimate private businesses increasing monthly, the problem of control has become an enormous one. The State Council has found itself in a perplexing double bind: the more economic freedom it grants, the more chaotic the situation becomes; and the more chaotic the situation becomes, the more it feels compelled to issue controls. Liao Jili, deputy general secretary of the State Economic System Reform Commission, in discussing the need to "invigorate" China's private microeconomy, observed in a year end report in 1982: "What we mean by 'invigoration' is 'invigoration' under unified-planning management, and within the scope permitted by the macroeconomy. This kind of 'invigoration' must conform to the demands of the macroeconomy; otherwise, 'invigoration' might become 'chaos.' "

By the end of 1982, there were 2.63 million private industrial and commercial enterprises licensed in China, involving nearly 3.25 million people. According to the State Administration Bureau for Industry and Commerce, by the beginning of 1984 this figure had more than doubled, to 5.86 million private industrial and commercial enterprises, which were employing over 7.5 million Chinese. While this is only a small percentage of China's population of more than a billion, the number of these businesses is growing rapidly, and already represents a more than sixtyfold increase over the number of such enterprises in existence five years ago.

By the beginning of 1984, the *China Daily* estimated that in Chongqing alone, the largest city in West China's Sichuan province, nearly 50,000 people were engaged in private trade in one of the city's 112 urban free markets. The paper noted that the 165,000 tons of food they sold in Chongqing during the first eleven months of 1983 was equal to 70 per cent of the total retail turnover in state-run food shops during the same period. Enterprising peasants from Sichuan had also found that they could make large profits by airlifting chickens and ducks to Lhasa and selling them to Tibetan buyers at premium prices. Nationwide, private businesses and free markets accounted for 10.2 per cent of all national retail sales, handling 71.2 per cent of all poultry sales, 31.1 per cent of egg, 30.5 per cent of beef and lamb, and 23.6 per cent of vegetable sales in the country as of 1984.

Although statistics-gathering in China is still a rather crude and politically self-serving art, such official figures—regardless of how they are gathered—do give an idea of where problems lie. And one of the major problems of regulating this new aspect of Chinese life is that China does not yet have the organization or the personnel in place to handle the job. In 1983, the Peking city government, for instance, had only fifty-six people to administer and regulate all the city's private retailers. With such a modest regulatory presence, it was not surprising to find the private sector rife with nefarious characters and illegal activity—what the Chinese press often refers to as "negative influences."

For example, a few days after I arrived in Peking in 1983, I came across a small item in the *China Daily* which reported that a group of workers at an electrical-machinery plant in Tianjin had been truant from their factory jobs in order to run their own fish-and-produce business. Plant managers had to order them to return, because the plant was failing to meet the year's production target. A check by Chinese authorities of individual retailers in Peking's Chongwen-district market area turned up 279 unlicensed individuals, 115 of whom were public employees playing hooky from their state jobs in order to sell illegally purchased clothes on the street.

When I asked a Chinese friend who works for a foreign electronics firm if his friends were now eager to go into business for themselves, he replied, "At first, none of them wanted to give up their iron rice bowls"—their guaranteed salary from a state job—"for something as uncertain as private business. Only unemployed youths found such a future at all tempting. But now, for the first time, people are beginning to look with a little more interest at the

prospect of going it alone, because they all know they w
get rich working in factories."

Factory workers with management training have begun
to consult on a private basis with small businesses that are
just starting up. Although the government has strict regulations against moonlighting, the promise of added income
often makes such activity irresistible. In fact, professionals
of many kinds, who up until now have worked on fixed
salaries for state enterprises, are beginning to discover that
their talents are highly marketable on the outside. A small
number have begun "to earn outside money" (*juan
waikuai*), or "to fly at night" (*chaogeng*).

Medical professionals like dentists and practitioners of
traditional Chinese medicine have received state approval
to set up private practices. However, some doctors trained
in Western medicine are also quietly seeing private patients
in order to supplement their state salaries. In July, 1983, a
doctor, Zhang Qu, in Yongji county, Zilin province, was reported in the Chinese press to have actually built a private
clinic with his own money and a bank loan which included
X-ray equipment, a pharmacy, inpatient facilities, a dining
room, and a garage. And, according to a friend who is an
economist at the Chinese Academy of Social Sciences' Institute of Economics, by 1983 consideration was also being given
to contracting out health clinics—which had been run by
collectives and state enterprises—to private management.
Calling for major reforms in China's health system, in a
March 11, 1984, article in the *People's Daily*—the principal
Party organ—Minister of Public Health Cui Yueli called for
(among other things), the breakup of the state's "monopoly"
on health care by encouraging other forms of service.

Teachers have also been moonlighting, giving cram
courses for students seeking to do well on the highly competitive university-entrance examinations. Jack M. Potter,
a professor of anthropology at the University of California
at Berkeley, who has been doing field work in southern

Guangdong province, reports that in his area teachers were being given salary increases or bonuses when their students gained admission to elite schools. Official approval has even been given to the establishment of privately run schools, which cater to those with money who fail to get into the state-run educational institutions. One of these new private schools is the Yanjing Foreign Languages Institute, in Peking, which in April of 1983 opened its doors to two hundred students; for an annual tuition of 250 yuan, students could study not only foreign languages but journalism as well. A few months later, Xinghua College, a private engineering school, also received permission to open from the Peking Educational Administration.

Another very lucrative private sideline activity in the Chinese countryside is entertainment. Singers, actors, opera troupes, storytellers, circuses, and film projection crews have begun to travel the countryside, providing shows for the peasants. On March 19, 1984, the *China Daily* reported that in Hunan province alone there were over two thousand independent peasant projection teams, which moved from village to village showing films for an admittance charge. In Magong, a small fishing port in Haifeng county, Guangdong province, Chen Sheng set another precedent in the privatization of entertainment when, using money he had saved and a private loan, he opened his own 550-seat movie theater.

Although such private entertainment companies have proliferated, conservative Chinese have been less than pleased with the results. Unlike the state-run troupes, which formerly had no pressure on them to fill their houses, private companies have to be ever mindful of how to maximize profits. And many of their entertainment programs have been criticized for being "unhealthy," for catering to the lowest instincts of those of their audience who like their shows sexy and *au courant*, or in Chinese parlance, *lu, tou,* and *guai*—"revealing," "translucent," and "weird."

The Chinese government has even granted approval for a privately owned shipping company to begin operating on the

Yangtze River. In the spring of 1984, the Min Sheng Shipping Company, a renowned private firm set up in Chongqing in 1926 by the Chinese entrepreneur and shipping magnate Lu Zhoufu, reopened its doors as a "privately run collective," with full control over its staff and administration under the leadership of Lu's sixty-one-year-old son.

In August, 1984, the *Liberation Daily*, a leading Shanghai paper, reported that a growing number of workers had been unsuccessfully trying to leave their jobs in state-run enterprises to work in the private sector. As one such man said, he was finding it "hard to fulfill his true potential in his present job." But what was more unusual than the report was the fact that *Liberation Daily* appeared to be berating the state-owned enterprises for not letting these ambitious pioneers leave in order to seek their fortune as workers in the private side of the economy.

Almost everywhere in China, people seemed fixated on their own well-being and making money. Even prisoners found themselves part of the new system in state-run jail workshops where promises of bonuses and higher pay for good behavior were introduced to increase production. Moreover, since this new application of the incentive system, officials at the Canton prison reported that no inmates had escaped.

Where all this was leading, no one knew. When I asked Chinese officials if there were limits beyond which the government would not allow the private sector to grow, I got nervous laughs and unconvincing assurances that everything was under control—that the private sector was still too small to be significant. The weekly news magazine *Beijing Review*, evidently concerned about the confusion that many of its readers were expressing over the role of a growing private sector in a socialist economy, published a short commentary in April of 1984 by its economic editor, Jin Qi. In it, he dismissed any suggestion that the system was beset by what Mao would have called an "antagonistic contradiction." "The private economy is subordinate to the socialist public economy, supplementing it in a very beneficial way," Jin wrote. "Those who believe that the growth of the private economy will change the current economic system have, to say the least, overlooked . . . basic facts."

From time to time, high-ranking officials gave speeches in which they attempted to grapple with the consequences of putting a capitalist fox into a socialist henhouse. "We must constantly watch out for the tendency in some works of literature and art toward crass commercialism regardless of the social consequences. This has already appeared and had a pernicious influence," Premier Zhao Ziyang warned a meeting of the National People's Congress in the spring of 1984. "We should adopt effective measures to rectify this tendency. For a considerably long time to come, we will strive to expand socialist production and commodity exchange, which . . . are essentially different from the profit-grabbing and anarchic commodity production characteristic of the capitalist system of private ownership. . . . In no case must we allow the decadent ideology of putting money above everything else to spread unchecked in our society."

In October, 1983, when the Party began a major campaign against "spiritual pollution and cultural contamination," and what Deng Liqun, head of the Central Committee's propaganda department, called "obscene, barbarous, or reactionary things," such as "efforts to seek personal gain, indulgences in individualism, anarchism, liberalism, etc.," one was left to wonder where Party officials thought all these poisonous tendencies were coming from. There was no suggestion that they might logically have some connection with the new economic policies. Like a gardener nipping off the tops of weeds and leaving the roots undisturbed, the Party seemed hopeful of rectifying the problem of "spiritual pollution" by requiring workers in the capital to undergo a couple of weeks of "ideological study."

But it was hard to imagine that such a measure would be effective. Most of the Chinese I met had become almost totally preoccupied with leading their own lives. Whether it was writing what the Party's monthly theoretical journal, *Red Flag*, referred to as "frivolous and depraved drama and literature," pursuing a career, or just making money, few Chinese had much energy left over for "ideological study." The private side of life had gained a momentum of its own, a momentum initiated by the Party itself. "It's as if a person who had carefully collected a box of marbles suddenly decided to spill them all out onto the middle of a wide street, where they could roll off in every direction," said one Western diplomat. "It's actually quite brave of the leadership. But it does make you wonder if they had any notion of how to control so many individuals all going their own different ways."

★

The people engaged in private business are not the only urban Chinese who have begun to profit financially from China's new economic policies. Most urban Chinese still work in state-owned enterprises, but their lives, too, have been profoundly affected. Prior to 1979, such enterprises operated as part of a planned and highly centralized Soviet-style system, which had been introduced into China during the fifties, the heyday of Sino-Soviet friendship. A factory producing drive shafts in Liaoning province, for instance, would be allotted a certain amount of raw material and told to produce a certain number of units by the appropriate ministry in Peking. Any profit had to be remitted to the central government. It was then up to the ministry to determine how much of that profit should be returned to the drive-shaft plant, in the form of subsidies for repairs, retooling, or expansion. Factory managers were essentially cogs in a machine controlled from above; workers were goaded by moral exhortations and political pressure rather than by material incentives.

But following the decisions of the Third Plenum, at the end of 1978, this system began to be radically changed.

Centralized control was relaxed, and state enterprises all across China were thrown back on their own resources, thus becoming more like privately owned factories in a capitalist economy. Under the new *zeren zhi*, or "responsibility system," the Liaoning drive-shaft factory was responsible for finding its own raw materials, setting its own production targets, and hiring and firing its own labor force instead of having to accept workers assigned by state labor bureaus. It no longer remitted its profits to a ministry; it retained them, after paying a tax, and made its own decisions about how those profits should be reinvested or spent. It also became responsible for its own losses. A factory worker had, for the first time in decades, opportunity for advancement, like his counterpart in the private entrepreneurial world. If he worked overtime, he received extra compensation. If the factory did well, he received a bonus. He was also made to feel more custodial toward his job, since if the factory was unprofitable—say, through the laziness of its work force or the incompetence of its managers—the government was no longer obligated to rescue it from bankruptcy with subsidies. As Qu Ming, secretary general of the State Council, put it in August, 1984, "The old pattern is no longer suited to the management and production of modern enterprises, [because] it severely limits the initiative of enterprise and workers."

Although, according to the Chinese, the value of the nation's gross industrial output for 1982—556 billion yuan —was 7 per cent higher than the 1981 figure, with heavy industry up 9.3 per cent and light industry up 5.6 per cent, and although later figures for the first three months of 1984 were reported to have risen again by 11.1 per cent and 10.9 per cent, major problems in industry continued. Among them was a dire shortage of well-trained technicians and managers. Many of China's factories were run by inept political appointees, who gained their positions during the Cultural Revolution, when "Redness" rather than "expertness" was the criterion. However, the Party was cleaning out these political anachronisms wherever possible.

Even the staid Peking Opera Theater began to conform to the new economic model. Zhao Yanxia, the company's reigning actress and the leader of its First Troupe, introduced aspects of the responsibility system in 1981. Formerly, her company of actors, singers, musicians, and dancers had been completely financed by the state; after 1981 only 70 per cent of her payroll came from government subsidies. The remaining 30 per cent came from the theater's box-office sales. Under the new system, members of the troupe received less pay when deficits occurred and a bonus when there were surpluses. Zhao reported to a *Beijing Review* correspondent that in the sixteen months since the experiment began, the company had shown an after-expenses profit of 247,000 yuan, which enabled the average performer to receive a monthly bonus of about 50 yuan. She said that the new system had definitely inspired her company to perform more conscientiously than when, in her words, they were "drowned in the sea of the big public pot."

"We realize more and more that if we do not remove the obstacles to the effective management of socialism, if we do not overcome the effects of leftist thinking, we cannot advance," Premier Zhao Ziyang told the National People's Congress in May, 1984, after announcing that the managers of China's 400,000 industrial enterprises would be granted even more leeway and authority to operate their plants free from state regulation and control. "We must encourage competition and prevent monopoly," Zhao added, referring not to the monopoly of big business, as in a capitalist society, but to the monopoly of the Chinese government itself.

Regionally run state-owned enterprises, like private businessmen, were quick to respond to this new clarion call for competition in the Chinese economy. For instance, in the spring of 1984, it was announced that CAAC (the Civil Aviation Administration of China)—China's state-run airline, which had acquired world renown for its chaotic management, filthy planes, and surly service—would no longer have a monopoly on air travel in China. Four new regional airlines were reported to be organizing companies of their own to enter the expanding market for air travel in China. The mayor of Shanghai, Wang Daohan, announced that municipal officials were negotiating with several foreign carriers to set up a joint venture for a new Shanghai airline. When asked what would happen to the CAAC monopoly, Mayor Wang said, "Monopoly should give way to competition." "A competitive business atmosphere will be a powerful spur to China's economic development, [even though] common sense tells us that where there is competition, there will be winners as well as losers," State Council spokesman Yuan Mu told a *China Daily* reporter in a 1984 interview, sounding almost indistinguishable from a nineteenth-century American capitalist.

Throughout 1984, the government began introducing more and more competition into the economy, not only by permitting private businesses and industries to be licensed but also by turning over small, unprofitable state-owned enterprises to private collectives. By May 1, for instance, Heilongjiang province in Manchuria had converted six hundred of these foundering enterprises from public to private management in the hope that autonomous management and capitalist incentives might revive them. By the middle of 1984, the State Council went so far as to call for cutting China's technology research institutes loose, forcing them to fend for themselves on a self-supporting basis without any government subsidies.

Not even the banks, once the most conservative of Chinese financial institutions, have stayed out of the competitive scramble for a profitable bottom line. Two Shanghai banks have set up lotteries to lure in more depositors. Like most other state enterprises in China, banks have now been put on a profit-and-loss basis. They are no longer subsidized by the government; their earnings come from interest on loans. But to have money to lend they must first entice depositors. In an attempt to win out over the competition, the Chinese People's Bank and the China Agricultural Bank linked up with the Shanghai No. 4 Radio Factory and the Shanghai No. 2 Television Factory to offer valuable prizes to depositors. Award nights turned into Shanghai events, with winners picked at elaborate ceremonies supervised by notary publics to assure that names were drawn impartially. But, like almost everything else in China these days, this lottery system soon underwent a rapid evolution into something more sophisticated. The giving away of radios and television sets was soon discontinued, because the two banks had discovered that they could get even more depositors simply by offering straight cash awards. For every 100,000 new accounts of at least sixty yuan, invested at the prevailing 3.24 per cent annual interest rate, each bank agreed to set up two new lotteries, promising to award five first prizes of four hundred yuan, ten second prizes of a hundred yuan, a hundred third prizes of twenty yuan, and ten thousand fourth prizes of two yuan. As a result of the lotteries, the report said, it was expected that monthly deposits would rise by 444 million yuan.

Notary publics were all but nonexistent in China during the Cultural Revolution, but they are now much in demand to manage a variety of business affairs. Private wealth resulting from the new economic policies has created a need for legal covenants, agreements, wills, and contracts, all of which require some sort of official witnessing or notarization. After the Communists came to power, there was virtually no need for wills, since few individuals had any wealth of consequence which could be inherited. But now that people have started to accumulate consumer goods, savings accounts, and expensive houses, inheritance has once again become a meaningful concept. Chinese law allows a person to will his estate to his heirs tax-free. To avoid family feuds over the authenticity of wills, many people are having them notarized. Ding Jianzhong, the head of the Peking municipal notary office, complained to the New China News Agency that in 1982 his staff of twenty-three had received more than eight thousand visitors, registered more than four thousand documents, and translated more than a thousand notarial papers. Notarial work "plays an important part in preventing disputes, reducing the number of lawsuits, and protecting public property and legitimate rights and interests of applicants," said Ding. "We have to redouble our efforts to meet increasing demand for notarial service."

Whether a redoubling of Ding's effort would have a noticeable effect on the workload of his office was debatable. The *Beijing Daily* reported that, in 1982, Chinese had signed more than 400 million new economic contracts, an astounding figure in view of the fact that only a few years earlier there had been virtually none. In 1983, these contracts generated some 7 million disputes which had to be resolved by China's 900,000 local mediation committees operating under the auspices of the Ministry of Justice's mediation department. But many disputes remained intractable and had to be litigated in China's new court system, to which the government found it necessary to appoint 10,000 new judges in one year in order to stay ahead of the caseload.

Moreover, in March of 1984, Zou Yu, China's Minister of Justice, complained to a visiting Belgian delegation that his country had only 15,000 full-time and part-time lawyers offering legal services, which meant that only about one per cent of China's enterprises—never mind its individual citizens—had any access to legal council. He said that his ministry was trying to train more lawyers to meet China's "increasingly pressing need" for legal advice.

The privatization of life has also spread into China's housing industry. A few short years ago, almost all of China's housing was built, owned, and managed by the state. But in 1983, the China Housing and Development Corporation chose five pilot cities and began building ten-thousand-yuan (five-thousand-U.S.-dollar) apartments for sale to private individuals. Those who did not have that much money in cash were encouraged to consider buying with a bank loan. "After sale, an apartment is private property," a spokesman for the corporation told the New China News Agency. The notion of "private property" may have been one to which he had gotten accustomed in his new job, but I must confess that it startled me when I came across his interview. It was the first time since I began studying China, in 1958, that I had seen a Chinese publication use the term in any but the most pejorative way.

By the beginning of 1984, Chinese news commentators were writing about the advantages of the government getting out of the housing business entirely. Responding to critics who protested that the average Chinese did not have enough savings to "buy" his own house, one writer suggested that the answer might be installment-plan buying. By spring 1984, what one Chinese reporter called "flat fever" hit China. In Chengdu the capital of Sichuan province, six hundred apartments were sold to private buyers during the first four months of the year. The New China News Agency boasted that more than five thousand private houses had been registered in the city since 1980. They even announced proudly that Deng Xiaoping himself had called for reforms that would take the construction of housing out of government hands and turn it into a profit-making industry.

China also began to build special luxury housing with telephones and air conditioning for overseas Chinese and for (as the New China News Agency put it) "former industrialists, businessmen, and senior intellectuals who need to improve their housing conditions." For instance, in March of 1984, the AJ Apartment Buildings, built by the Shanghai Patriotic Construction Corporation and offering such upscale apartments, were put on the market in Shanghai and sold out almost immediately.

With private business and private property now playing an integral part in everyday life, many Chinese have become concerned about protecting their assets against loss, whether from fire, flood, or theft. This concern has caused a sudden boom in the domestic insurance market. The People's Insurance Company of China, which wrote virtually no such policies before the recent changes in government policy, reported that its income from domestic insurance premiums —most of it coming from policies taken out on private-collective enterprises, private businesses, family property, and motor vehicles—rose more than 36 per cent in 1983, to over one billion yuan. By July of 1984, 2.57 million Chinese had reportedly bought life insurance policies, and the People's Insurance Company of China, having already expanded its operations to include 1,600 branch offices, was about to add another 13,000 employees to its existing staff of 20,000 and open for business in Tibet.

Another institution from the *ancien régime* which has made a surprising comeback in China is the tax code. Once proud of itself as a socialist society that was so progressive it did not need an elaborate tax system, China now is frantically trying to build an enormous new tax-collecting bureaucracy. Since individuals are allowed a deduction of eight hundred yuan a month, scarcely anyone pays a personal income tax, but substantial revenues are anticipated from corporate taxes. The new corporate-tax system, which went into effect in June, 1983, was necessitated not only by the appearance of so many private businesses, from which the state hoped to derive revenue, but by the fact that most state-owned businesses no longer handed over their profits directly to the state. Businesses that make more than 200,000 yuan in annual profits must now pay a 55 per cent tax to the Ministry of Finance's Tax Office. Smaller businesses are taxed on an eight-grade scale. By the summer of 1983, China reportedly had 4.2 million domestic taxable enterprises, over three-quarters of them privately owned.

Wondering how a newly created bureaucracy in such a vast and underdeveloped country as China could ever ride herd on so many potential taxpayers, I went to talk with

Jamie P. Horsley, an attorney with the New York law firm of Paul, Weiss, Rifkind, Wharton and Garrison, who practices in Peking and has closely studied the Chinese tax laws. "The new tax system is just one of many extraordinary changes," she told me. "The whole economic situation here has been moving so quickly that it's often difficult to keep up with it. With this new system, the Chinese are attempting not only to create a bureaucracy out of nothing but to educate all the people who will be paying these taxes. It's an enormous undertaking. And, knowing firsthand how confused they have been in implementing a program to tax foreigners and foreign businesses, I'm not at all sure they're going to have an easy time of it. It will be difficult enough for them to collect taxes in the cities, but in the countryside I think compliance problems will be staggering."

Horsley had been leafing through some files as we talked, and she handed me a clipping to look at. It was a translation of a letter to the *People's Daily* from an official named Wang Jing, who worked in the Ministry of Finance's Tax Office. In the letter, Wang claimed that the tax-collection system was already being given a hostile reception. He reported that since its establishment there had been 270 incidents involving assaults on tax collectors by "criminal elements"; in some cases, the collectors had been paraded through the streets to be publicly mocked. "Tax collectors do not receive powerful support from local public-security and judicial organs," Wang complained in his letter. "In many instances, because criminal elements resisted taxes of less than a thousand yuan, judicial organs won't bother with the case, and hoodlums who beat up tax collectors become more and more arrogant, because they don't receive the punishment they should."

"This sort of situation was more or less where the Nationalists left off in the nineteen-forties," Horsley said. "Whether the system will eventually function well or not is open to question. But one thing that's becoming evident is that taxes are beginning to have a significant effect on the way business is done in China. As the local press frankly reports, taxation is being accompanied by widespread tax fraud and evasion."

★

Although China under the Communists has never been as free of crime as many visiting Westerners supposed, a pronounced upsurge of criminal activity in the early 1980s caused concern even among the highest echelons of the Chinese leadership. In January of 1982, the Party launched a nationwide anti-crime campaign. Chinese newspapers, which once were filled with slogans and long theoretical tracts, became so peppered with lurid accounts of crime and corruption that at times they read like tabloids; the object of such news stories was not to titillate or to sell papers but to warn offenders that criminal activity would be severely dealt with. *Red Flag* deplored the existence of "elements hostile to the socialist system," who "rob the state of property, kill and maim the nation's workers at their posts, hijack, rape women, traffic in women and children, tyrannize others, [and] trample upon the masses." Well into the campaign, China's Minister of Public Security, Liu Fuzhi, announced that, in 1982, 750,000 street crimes had been reported—an average of 7.5 for every 10,000 people. (Whatever one might make of the figures or their accuracy, the announcement itself was unusual, since the Chinese government rarely divulges information that might embarrass the Communist Party.) The incidence of street crime had been rising, officials admitted, since 1956, when the rate was officially reported to be as low as 2.3 per 10,000.

A year after the anti-crime campaign began, the first publicized executions occurred. Wang Zhong, the fifty-six-year-old Party secretary of Guangdong's Haifeng county, was executed on January 17, 1983, by a pistol shot in the back of the head, for defrauding the state of about 70,000 yuan and for taking bribes from people who wanted to escape to Hong Kong. (The *People's Daily* called Wang's execution "most gratifying news.") The following day, a second Guangdong man—Li Jingfang, aged fifty-five—was executed for embezzling more than 600,000 yuan from a local bank.

When I arrived in China that summer, the anti-crime publicity campaign was just getting into high gear. According to one report, an increase in the number of executions was ordered by Deng Xiaoping himself, who had recently encountered a pack of gangsters on a highway near the coastal town of Beidaihe while travelling in a motorcade with President Li Xiannian; one of the President's aides had been slashed with a knife. Almost every other day, it seemed, there was a story in the newspapers about gangs. They were active even in the remote reaches of Inner Mongolia, where a gang known as the Bridgehead Squad, whose members had eagles tattooed on their left arms, was arrested in August. In the city of Tangshan, in Hebei province, six different gangs, consisting of more than a hundred criminals, were rounded up, arrested, and accused of murder, assault, ransacking people's houses, robbery, and "insulting women in public places." Many of the gang members were ex-inmates of labor camps, in which "antisocial elements" can be incarcerated without a trial. Another gang sentenced while I was in Peking had had its headquarters in the city of Anyang, in Henan province, but had expanded its operations throughout three nearby provinces, kidnapping young women and selling them, for up to nine hundred yuan each, to peasants who could not find wives. Before the gang was broken up and arrested, in November of 1982, it had reportedly kidnapped and sold more than 150 women. The leader was sentenced to death, and thirty gang members received prison terms ranging from ten to twenty years.

The most celebrated gangsters of 1983 were the Wang brothers. Wang Zongfang and Wang Zongwei were two men in their twenties who roamed back and forth across

China by train, committing robberies, shooting their way out of trouble, and living by their wits. They were said to be heavily armed and to have killed fifteen people. For months, the Wang brothers eluded security forces, travelling all the way from their home, in Shenyang, Manchuria, south to Guangdong province, where they unsuccessfully tried to escape to Hong Kong. The police became so frustrated at not being able to apprehend the brothers that they finally offered cash rewards and put up "wanted" posters, complete with photographs. I spotted one of these posters on a bulletin board in downtown Peking; a small crowd had gathered to have a look. Above brief descriptions were photographs of two handsome young faces wearing half-smiles, as though for the pages of a high school yearbook. Having expected to see rough, sneering countenances like those on the FBI's "most wanted" posters in American post offices, I found the well-groomed Wang brothers—with their open-necked white sports shirts and pleasant expressions—a bit of a surprise. After a while, I got into conversations with a young student who seemed quite spellbound by the brothers. They had "a lot of guts," he said. When I asked him if he would like to collect a reward, he replied wryly, "Why not? Catching criminals has now become part of the material-incentive system."

When I raised the subject of the Wang brothers with Chinese thereafter, I found that, far from being outraged by their lawlessness, many people were fascinated, even sympathetic. The unusual ability of these two young men to evade the power of the state had imbued them with heroic dimensions; many Chinese, apparently, longed to see their system, including the dreaded Public Security Bureau, bested. Like the invincible bandit heroes of the sixteenth-century adventure novel *The Water Margin* (best known in the West in Pearl Buck's translation, *All Men Are Brothers*), whom almost all Chinese idolize, the Wang brothers had become romantic legends. In September, however, they were finally tracked down and killed by security forces after a fierce gun battle in a mountain hideout in Jiangxi province.

The anti-crime campaign received a big boost in July, 1983, when the Party's Central Commission for Discipline Inspection issued a special report entitled *On the Work of Striking at Serious Crimes in the Economic Field*. It was publicized throughout China after being presented to the National People's Congress by the commission's secretary, Han Guang. In a speech on that occasion, Han listed the major crimes plaguing China. They included "large-scale smuggling; tax evasion; illicit trade in foreign exchanges, goods, and materials by personnel of government agencies, enterprises, or institutions; large-scale speculation and fraud by unlawful elements; embezzlement; accepting bribes and theft by state employees, including a few leading Party cadres; organized smuggling of precious cultural relics, gold, silver, rare gems, and medicinal herbs out of China, as well as smuggling of large amounts of industrial goods, narcotics, pornographic materials, and reactionary publications into China; [and] indiscriminate hiring of veteran criminals by [state-run] enterprises in the belief that they are good at making money."

He went on to give some rather shocking statistics. From January 1, 1982, until April 30, 1983, 192,000 cases of economic crime—involving, among others, 71,000 Party members—had come to light. With investigations in three-quarters of the cases completed, over 400 million yuan in embezzled goods and "illicit money" had been recovered. The report described the criminals as "termites undermining the edifice of socialism [who] cause tremendous damage to economic construction, upset social stability, debase the standards of social conduct, and corrupt people's minds and lives." In early September, in an effort to deal with such "termites" severely and swiftly, the Standing Committee of the National People's Congress expediently revised the new criminal code. Defendants now had less time to appeal their convictions; it was no longer required that two "members of the masses" assist the judge in his decision; and the death penalty could be imposed for a wider variety of offenses, including those which, in the eyes of the authorities, "seriously endanger public security." It was not long before reports, even in the Chinese press, began to appear, accusing overly zealous officials of making wrongful arrests and of using torture to extract confessions.

To deter crime the government began publicly sentencing large numbers of criminals to death at "prosecution rallies." On August 23, 1983, the Public Security Bureau held a rally at a Peking sports stadium, at which twenty-nine men and one woman were paraded in front of a cheering crowd before being taken away to be executed for their criminal activities. In the weeks that followed, the names of numerous other criminals were marked with red checks on posters displayed in front of the courthouses all over China—a sign that they, too, had been sentenced to death. One of those who received the death sentence in the summer of 1983 was the grandson of the renowned Marshal Zhu De, a general who had fought alongside Mao since the nineteen-twenties. Zhu Guohua, a Tianjin railroad worker, was accused of leading a ring of thieves who had reportedly gang-raped thirty women, and of using the name of his famous grandfather to avoid arrest. He was put to death in September, along with eighty-one other sons and grandsons of Army officers, in what proved to be the largest mass execution of the anticrime campaign to date.

A report in the Hong Kong magazine *Cheng Ming* early in February, 1984, claimed that another of Zhu De's grandsons, Zhu Yuanchao, was spared the death penalty for committing grave economic crimes only because some Chinese leaders thought that to execute two close relatives of the renowned marshal would be an insult to his memory. The same report also claimed that a grandnephew of President Li Xiannian had been executed in Xi'an, Shaanxi province, for rape and murder, and that the son of Deputy Foreign

Minister Yao Guang had been arrested in the capital for smuggling pornography.

When I arrived in Taicheng, the seat of rural Taishan county, Guangdong province, in January of 1984, billboards and walls in public places had been plastered with anti-crime posters for several months. Printed in black on large sheets of white paper, the posters showed mug shots of criminals alongside brief descriptions of who they were and what offenses they had committed. Those criminals ultimately executed had bold red X's slashed across their faces.

In smaller towns in Taishan and neighboring counties, there seemed to be hardly any upright surface facing onto a main street which was not covered with these posters. The older ones, from the first waves of roundups and executions, had faded crimson X's and were tattered and gray. The more recent ones, however, gleamed out brightly, reminding passers-by that the job of the Chinese judicial system was, at present, not so much delivering justice as making examples of wrongdoers and deterring future crimes.

Whenever new posters went up, an ever-changing crowd of people would gather in front of them. At one busy street corner in Taicheng, the county government had organized a display of eight-by-ten glossy anti-crime photographs set in a glass case that in different times might have been used for propaganda on hygiene or for directives from the local Party branch. But now it was filled with grainy photographs of grim-looking youths gone wrong and of blindfolded convicts awaiting execution with bowed heads and hands bound behind their backs. There was only one female face in this rogues' gallery: that of a middle-aged woman accused of luring girls into prostitution.

One afternoon, while passing the Taicheng Youth Cultural Palace, a complex of buildings consecrated to "youth activities," I noticed a sign announcing yet another anti-crime effort—an exhibit that had opened inside the day before. Walking into the courtyard around which the Cultural Palace was constructed, I saw lines of students on school field trips waiting to enter the exhibit hall. When I myself tried to enter, I was told by a guard at the door that it was "inconvenient for foreign guests" to view the exhibit at that time, and that I should return later.

Wandering around the courtyard, I passed a series of exhortatory placards, which the Chinese Communists tirelessly produce in the hope of spurring their youth on to nobler and more selfless lives. One placard bore a picture of a red rose and the caption BE A MORAL PERSON. But just how this particular cultural palace was contributing to the process of making Chinese youth "moral" was difficult to understand, since the main visible youth activity there was pool. Three large pool halls were filled with questionable-looking young men and dense clouds of cigarette smoke. Peering into one of these gloomy halls, I spotted more placards. One bore a quotation from Lenin: IF ONE DOES NOT REST, ONE CANNOT WORK. Opposite it hung a placard bearing a slightly different message, attributed to the renowned Chinese writer Lu Xun. It reminded the roomful of pool-playing youths: IF ONE WISHES TO ATTAIN CULTURAL ACHIEVEMENT, ONE MUST WORK HARD.

It was not until the next day that I succeeded in getting into the anti-crime exhibit. It was on the second floor of another dark and gloomy building, and consisted of expositions of crimes told in comic-book fashion, partially through photographs and partially through a series of lurid artists' renderings in color. One sequence showed how a middle-aged man had preyed upon a superstitious young woman by convincing her that he could cure her of an illness if she had sex with him. Another chronicled the kidnapping of a peasant girl by a man who sexually abused her, and then took her to a distant county to sell her into bondage. A third portrayed events surrounding a family feud and murder. A fourth depicted the case of a young man who was convicted of smuggling and illegally selling goods.

As if to prove beyond the shadow of a doubt that the crimes were real, the artists had included in their paintings a liberal number of bright red pools of blood, dripping knives and cleavers, and guns and clubs. The criminals themselves were portrayed as skulking, devious-looking figures with ratty hair and rumpled clothing. Their faces were sallow and hard and wore expressions of unrepentant evil. The Party cadres and Security Bureau police, on the other hand, were portrayed as righteous and incorruptible, their ruddy faces replete with indignation as they glowered down at the unsavory "bad elements" they were arresting. The distinction between these socialist superheroes and the criminals was rendered in a manner so stark that even the youngest child could not fail to distinguish which side was which.

In another section of the hall there were photographs of pornographic video cassettes, tape recorders, cameras, and ghetto blasters illegally smuggled in from Hong Kong, which shares a common border with Guangdong province. There were also photographs of houses, villages, and deserted country glades where the victims of these publicized crimes had been robbed, raped, kidnapped, and murdered.

Several days after visiting the anti-crime exhibit, I was walking early one morning in the streets of Taicheng when I suddenly started to see columns of students marching by, laughing and talking. After at least a thousand had passed, I was quite curious about where they were going and what they were doing out of school en masse on a weekday morning. Following one long line, I found that they were marching through the gates of a large athletic field beside the Tungji River, which flows by the edge of town. At one end of the field was a bandstand decked out with anti-crime banners. One of Taicheng's pre-execution rallies was scheduled to begin in half an hour.

Rushing back to the center of town, I learned that a parade of criminals being taken to the rally would commence momentarily. No sooner had I loaded my camera than I saw a phalanx of white-jacketed Security Bureau policemen heading down the main street, shouting at pedestrians to clear the way. Never have I seen a busy street in China empty so quickly, or experienced the kind of eerie silence that hushed the crowd that morning.

Moments after the police sweep, a procession of open-backed Army trucks appeared in the distance and inched slowly toward us as people in the sidewalk arcades craned their necks to get a better view. In the back of the first truck stood a single grim-faced young man, hands bound behind his back, head lowered. Around his neck hung a white placard listing his offense and name, which was slashed with the familiar crimson X. As the truck slowly passed, I could see the face of the young criminal, wearing a haunting expression that mixed resignation with terror.

Three more trucks passed, carrying three more criminals condemned to death. All wore placards around their necks emblazoned with crimson X's. Then came three more trucks, filled with ten or more criminals, each of whom had been convicted of non-capital offenses, their lesser crimes evidently not giving them sufficient status in the world of anti-crime campaign symbology to warrant a private vehicle.

Bringing up the rear of this macabre procession were two more trucks filled with young militiamen, rifles slung over their shoulders and faces frozen in expressions of righteous defiance every bit as stylized as those of their counterparts in the anti-crime exhibit. The very last vehicle in this strange psychodrama was filled with People's Liberation Army soldiers in full uniform, the two soldiers in front bracing machine guns on the cab of the truck as if at any moment they expected trouble from their securely bound charges. Only after the whole cavalcade had passed half a block beyond did a murmur go up from the crowd.

Hurrying back to the rally ground, I could already hear the sound of martial music drifting out across Taicheng. Then as I approached the gates of the field, it suddenly stopped and a strident voice began blasting out over a loudspeaker. The students, thousands of them, were all sitting quietly on the ground with basketball nets, soccer goals, and other sports-field paraphernalia arrayed around them. The prisoners remained in their trucks, which had been parked next to the bandstand where they could be seen by all as the speeches droned on.

"How many have they shot already?" I whispered to a youth, who looked very uneasy at the thought of my presence. At first he did not answer. Then, glancing around with wary eyes, he replied, "Ten that I know of. But there have been more in the countryside." That said, he darted away with the swiftness of a frightened trout. Moments later a very agitated Security Bureau policeman approached me and said, in halting but menacing English, "Go out! Go out!" and pointed toward the gate.

That evening I met a twenty-two-year-old soldier who had just been demobilized in another part of China. As we walked the dark streets of Taicheng, he told me how, after the rally, two of the condemned men had been taken back to their rural villages to be executed among their own people. The other two condemned men had been led down to the riverbank, blindfolded, forced to kneel, and then shot in the back of the neck while a thousand or so onlookers—this young soldier among them—lingered to watch.

When I asked why the authorities allowed people to watch, he laughed and said, "They want us to. They want to scare people and make a big point." He was silent for a moment, and then added, somewhat hesitantly, "There's an old custom here in China, and they've revived it again. After a criminal has been shot, his family is sent a bill of twenty-five cents for the bullet. It's a reminder that a criminal not only brings punishment on himself but shame on the whole family in which he was raised."

As early as mid-October of 1983, foreign diplomats in Peking were estimating that between 1,000 and 2,000 people had been executed throughout China since the campaign began. They reported that Chinese internal documents called for a quota of 5,000 executions and 50,000 arrests by the end of the year. However, by January of 1984, many Western correspondents were coming to believe that the figure was actually much higher. Tiziano Terzani, Peking bureau chief for the German news weekly *Der Spiegel*, who was later expelled from China for his outspoken articles, calculated that the figure was closer to 15,000 executed.

These Draconian measures appear to have been at least temporarily effective: the government announced at the beginning of January, 1984, that the crime rate in the closing months of 1983 was down by 40 per cent compared with the same period in 1982, and that for the first six months of 1984, it was down almost 50 per cent. Nonetheless, throughout 1984 reports of gang activity continued to circulate, including accounts about the "five fingers" and "two wolves," seven gang leaders in the city of Beian, Heilongjiang province. When they and their gangs, made up largely of the sons of high-ranking cadres, were arrested after a knife fight with a policeman at a Beian restaurant, they stood accused of no less than three hundred crimes of rape and violence.

The Party blamed the upsurge of crime on the "chaotic" years of the Cultural Revolution, when young people went undisciplined, and on "bourgeois influences" that had slipped into China as a result of its new open-door policy. What Party officials seem to have overlooked was that the "bourgeois influences" were in many respects part and parcel of the reformed economic system, which they themselves had instituted and continued to extoll. Unemployment had left millions of youths loose on the streets of Chinese cities. In the countryside, people were no longer tied to their registered address, or *hukou*, by the need for government coupons for grain, oil, and cotton products. With new wealth and peasant-run free markets everywhere, such coupons were no longer indispensable. People could buy what they needed wherever they wanted, and were thus freed from the tightly organized system that once held them firmly in place. Criminals could move about with ease. And the new private sector or economy had opened a netherworld for criminals in China— a Sherwood Forest within the king's domain, into which outlaws, like Robin Hood's Merry Men, could retreat and live. Here, in the middle of organized Chinese society, criminals were able to survive and carry on the pursuit of individual wealth, which the Chinese leadership itself now glorified.

★

"Oh, yes. Absolutely. Things in the countryside have definitely changed for the better," a Chinese friend who works for a research arm of the State Council told me with smiling confidence one evening in Peking. "Previously, the Chinese peasants relied too much on the Party and on the government. They didn't really have to exert themselves or bear any responsibility for their lives. They had no incentive to do so. They always knew they would eat regardless of how much work they did."

When urban Chinese speak about the situation in the countryside, "incentive" is a word that occurs over and over, like a leitmotiv. The idea of offering economic incentives to peasants was unthinkable until the Third Plenum of the Eleventh Party Central Committee met, in December, 1978, and changed the whole course of China's economy; now economic incentives are considered not only very effective but ideologically correct as well. "Since peasants have been given the incentive to get rich, production has shot up," my friend continued, fairly sparkling with optimism. "I think we may say that at last China has found the internal force it needs to push development forward in the countryside."

Although the Communist Chinese have always idealized the peasantry as the engine of the Revolution, urban Party members have in fact never been very enthusiastic about the idea of rural life. Like their precursors, the Confucian scholar-officials of Imperial times, contemporary educated

Chinese look upon peasant labor as uncivilized and beneath their dignity. More than two thousand years ago, Mencius, a disciple of Confucius, articulated their feelings: "Some labor with their brains and some labor with their brawn. Those who labor with their brains govern others. Those who labor with their brawn are governed by others. Those governed by others feed them. Those who govern others are fed by them. This is a universal principle in the world." Communist pronunciamentos notwithstanding, this spirit lives on in the People's Republic.

Mao Zedong, who was from a peasant family, was keenly aware of the vast chasm dividing rural and urban China. (The Communists came to call it the "Three Great Differences": mental-manual, worker-peasant, city-country.) He also knew that arrogant intellectuals were clinging to their privileged positions in the cities, where they could enjoy comfort, culture, wealth, power, and opportunity. To bridge the division between urban and rural China, Mao sent millions of city people to the countryside, some for many years, to take part in *laogai*, or "reform through labor." For most of them, being marooned in the backwardness of rural China was a painful and bitter experience. But in the last three or four years the new economic reforms have quite unexpectedly begun to alter the nature of the traditional relationship between city and countryside. The changes that have come to China's 800 million peasants rival even those of the monumental collectivization of land in the nineteen-fifties. A surprising number of China's earthbound peasants are becoming wealthy. Perhaps for the first time in Chinese history, some city dwellers are starting to view certain of their country cousins with a degree of envy.

The backbone of Chinese collectivized agriculture had been the 50,000 people's communes, which were set up, at Mao's urging, in 1958 and 1959, during the Great Leap Forward. Varying widely in size from a few thousand to 60,000 or 70,000 members, the communes served as administrative units that organized large-scale irrigation and land-conservation projects, maintained heavy farm equipment, ran factories and hydroelectric plants, and provided health, education, and welfare services to the old and the indigent. They were composed of a patchwork of production brigades, which were made up of anywhere from a hundred to a couple of thousand people and were usually built around one or more pre-existing villages. The brigades managed smaller industries and agricultural operations, and occasionally provided basic elementary education, child-care services, and simple health-care facilities. The lowest level of rural organization was the production team, which consisted of twenty or thirty households. Teams collectively farmed fields assigned by the brigades and served as the basic accounting unit, seeing that each member received a salary and a share of the common harvest according to the number of "work points" he or she had been awarded by team comrades. Each administrative level was dominated by cadres appointed by the Party to assure that production quotas were met and that political decisions coming down the chain of command were implemented.

Like urban factory workers, individual peasants were pawns in the collective system, exercising no decision-making power of their own except over small private plots, which were periodically allowed and disallowed as different political winds swept over the leadership in Peking. A peasant's duty was to "build socialism," and to labor for the collective rather than for himself or his family. Having worked in the model Dazhai brigade in Shanxi province in 1975, during the ascendancy of the Gang of Four, I have vivid memories of how chillingly regimental life was. There were endless political meetings. At that time, peasants were not permitted to raise chickens or ducks of their own, much less cultivate private plots. All work was done collectively, with commonly owned tools. Any suggestion that one harbored deviant thoughts brought ostracism from the Party cadres, who watched over every aspect of brigade life with suffocating scrutiny.

Soon after I first returned to Peking in the summer of 1983, I gathered that this description of the countryside was no longer even remotely accurate. I say "gathered" because, unlike China's cities, which have been almost completely opened up to foreign travel, the countryside is still closed, and can usually be visited only by special permit or on short trips that are carefully organized by the government. Until I succeeded in getting into several rural areas of China in January, 1984, my attempts to fathom what was going on in the countryside from Peking were a little like the efforts of an army commander to put together a picture of a large battle raging outside the city walls from the communiqués he can receive at headquarters. Everywhere in the city, one heard stories via the amazing Chinese grapevine, which does more to keep people in China informed than the media and one's own observations combined.

When I asked the anthropologist Jack Potter about his impressions of the Chinese countryside in Guangdong province, he spoke of his experience with some awe: "When I first visited the Zengbu brigade there, in 1979, there was virtually nothing in the market. When I went back in 1981, things had started to pick up. But when I returned in 1983 I couldn't believe what I saw. There were hundreds of people selling things. There were tanks of live fish, and piles of fruit and vegetables heaped up everywhere. Lots of pigs were being slaughtered for meat—something you rarely would have seen in the past. You could buy Coca-Cola, Budweiser beer, and foreign cigarettes at private shops. The prosperity was impressive."

In January, 1984, on my trip to Taishan county in Guangdong province—where I had witnessed the execution rally—I finally got a chance to visit a rural market town myself. What I encountered by way of private enterprise made the free markets of Peking and other northern cities seem like comparative sideshows. Being adjacent to the colonies of Hong Kong and Macao, Taishan was way ahead of most of the rest of China in private commercial development. Even on normal non-market days, the main streets of Taicheng were lined with hundreds of booths and peddlers selling everything from clothing, household goods, and hardware to produce and wild animals. But at official market times—every fifth day—the number of private merchants swelled into the thousands. From early in the morning until dusk, the four main roads leading into town were filled with peasants coming in from the countryside with their produce on bicycles, carts drawn by hand tractors, trucks, and public buses. Once in Taicheng, they choked the streets with their booths and displays of goods, creating several strata of commercial activity.

The first stratum included those merchants who physically occupied shop space on the ground floor of buildings facing the streets. Once owned and run by the state, a significant number of these commercial spaces had now been leased out to private management, so that many dry-goods shops, pharmacies, restaurants, bakeries, furniture stores, beauty salons, and groceries were now run privately. Only the largest stores, such as those selling expensive machinery and appliances, fertilizer, or grain, and those large department stores that maintain a general inventory, were still state-run.

The next stratum of private commercial activity was located on the sidewalks right in front of these shops under the protection of their overhanging arcades. In this group one could find letter writers, barbers, watch and electronic-appliance repairmen, knife sharpeners, and tailors, who sat at small home-made workbenches. The third stratum was composed of a cordon of merchants who had regular booths constructed out of bamboo with roofs made of scraps of tar paper and old plastic fertilizer bags. These were permanently situated just outside the sheltering arcades on the side streets.

Just in front of these booths one found an assortment of small-time mobile peddlers who had simply arrived in town, unfolded a drop cloth, and were now displaying their wares to customers right on the street. Finally, in the very middle of the passing crowds in the streets, creating an effect of stones in a fast-moving stream, stood medicine peddlers who raucously hawked their dubious tonics and potions to clumps of curious people in the style of burlesque-house barkers.

Although the Taicheng outdoor market extends over a large part of the town and at first glimpse appears somewhat chaotically arranged, after one has walked in it for a few days its inner logic reveals itself. Just like a Western supermarket that groups like products together—detergents and floor wax, eggs and dairy products, fruits and vegetables, mayonnaise, ketchup, and other condiments—so peddlers selling similar things in the Taicheng street market generally congregated in one place. For instance, on one side street the merchants all displayed racks of brightly colored leisure suits and designer jeans. It was a disorienting feeling to walk down a street full of earthbound Chinese peasants in their rough, padded jackets and see clothing with labels like Murjani, Esprit, Silver Jet, and Autumn Attitudes for sale all around them. (On another street, where shoes and luggage were sold, a long-haired youth in a Western-style jacket manned a booth with a colorful display of plastic shopping bags bearing such inscriptions as "Nantucket," "Daytona Beach" and "I Love the Big Apple.")

There was a special area in the market for peasants selling live chickens, ducks, and geese. Those farmers who sold unrationed grain gathered on their own stretch of street. Peasants selling pork, beef, and fish occupied a special roofed-over area in the center of the market.

A unique section of the market was a stretch of street where wild animals were sold, or what an American friend of mine came to call the "gourmet meat section." Here one could buy live owls, hawks, songbirds, rats, monkeys, lizards, frogs, snakes, badgers, weasels, wildcats, and assorted other exotic animals that can be profitably trapped and sold by peasants because many Chinese believe their ingestion bestows longevity or increases their virility. In fact, so severe has the depletion of certain species of wild predators such as owls, hawks, and snakes become that in March, 1984, the Ministry of Forestry's wildlife protection department warned the country of a new problem: the rodent population was reaching dangerous proportions. These officials estimated that rodents annually destroyed five million tons of grain, ruined large numbers of young trees, and devoured millions of tons of fodder already in short supply. But if the Chinese in the Taicheng market were concerned about or even aware of such long-range problems, there was no evidence of it. As long as there was money to be made, wild animals would be sold.

One day, disheartened by the sight of all the hawks and large, beautiful owls waiting in the market to be bought and eaten, my friend and I bought three or four cagefuls, took them to a remote reservoir, and let them go. Returning to the market the next day, we were accosted anew by the owl and hawk salesmen, who had replenished their supply overnight. Evidently convinced now that foreigners had an inexhaustible appetite for owls and hawks, they ran up to us in the streets with cages of freshly caught birds, which they were now willing to sell at discount prices if once again we purchased in quantity.

All the produce in the Taicheng market had been grown privately, and reflected the dramatic change through which Chinese agriculture was passing. Virtually the entire fabric of Maoist ideology and the legacy of agricultural collectivization had been discarded as "leftist errors." A Party theoretician named Hu Sheng attempted an explanation in an article published in *Red Flag* in the spring of 1983: "During the Cultural Revolution, China's situation was wrongly assessed, and it was believed that bourgeois reactionary forces were ubiquitous. Worse still, the wrong conclusion was made that the status quo could be changed and the 'purest' and 'most perfect' socialist society established with one or two thrusts of the mass struggle. All these, needless to say, are utopian ideas, which brought nothing . . . but harm." Though "utopian ideas" were once the heart and soul of the Chinese Revolution, they have now been dismissed as, in Hu's words, "abstract concepts" that are "estranged from reality." What was once esteemed as "correct" thought is now viewed as "erroneous." The communes, which seemed an unalterable part of rural life, have begun to be dismantled, and the brigades and teams have been depoliticized. Chairman Mao appears to have been stood on his head.

As in industry, what replaced the Maoist way of doing things in agriculture was the "responsibility system." In his recent book, *New Strategy for China's Economy*, Ma Hong, the president of the Chinese Academy of Social Sciences, observed: "In the past, we overemphasized collective leadership and slighted individual responsibility; the result was that everyone was nominally responsible but no one actually assumed responsibility. This has now begun to change." When I asked an elderly peasant guarding a heap of watermelons he had brought in from the countryside to sell at a market in Peking what was meant by the responsibility system, he furrowed his brow at first, and then a pleased smile creased his face. "It means we can do what we want," he replied.

Probably the most startling aspect of the responsibility system is the decollectivization of land. The people's communes have ceased to exist. In the words of a Ministry of Civic Affairs official to a *China Daily* reporter, "They are no longer suited to further development of the rural economy." Although still owned by the state, land has been divided up into small plots and contracted out by the brigades to be farmed privately under a program referred to as *baochan daohu*, or "fixing farm-output quotas for individual households." A peasant's only binding obligation, besides paying rent and a small agricultural tax, is to deliver a fixed annual quota of grain to the state at a controlled price. Before the program was fully under way, this price was quite low, but in March of 1979, to help stimulate agriculture, the government raised the price of quota grain by 20 per cent and of grain exceeding the quota by 50 per cent. It also increased the prices it would pay for eighteen other principal agricultural products, by 25 per cent. Almost overnight, signs of new prosperity appeared in rural China. In his speech to the National People's Congress in the spring of 1983, Premier Zhao Ziyang proudly told the delegates that the responsibility system had "fired the enthusiasm of hundreds of millions of Chinese peasants and provided a powerful stimulus to production."

Peasants, who may own houses if not land, began an orgy of home-building with their new wealth. In the rural areas surrounding Peking, for instance, peasant housing increased 25 per cent from 1978 to 1982. This craze for house-building is not restricted to rich peasants, either. While in Peking during the winter of 1984, I learned to my surprise that one Chinese acquaintance, who already occupied a spacious apartment in Peking, had built himself a "second home," a private retreat next to a small lake about a half-hour from the capital, using a lump sum of money with which the state had reimbursed him for property confiscated from his family during the Cultural Revolution. This particular Peking bachelor had succeeded in negotiating a long-term lease with a peasant who did not wish to farm all the land he had been allotted under his responsibility-system contract. When I went out to see the house one cold January afternoon, my friend told me with pride how he had even gotten the peasant's local work brigade to approve the lease, and then gone on to hire a private contractor to build the house to his specifications, which called for two bedrooms, a large kitchen, a Western-style bathroom, a sun deck, and a central room about twenty by thirty feet in size.

The construction of small buildings and private houses in rural China is usually done by a private builder, or "boss" (*tou*), who in turn, for a percentage of the building contract price, hires the masons, carpenters, and laborers to do the work. In many parts of China the demand for these independently run construction crews is so great that they are booked up months in advance. A good "boss" can make ten to twenty thousand yuan a year if he can manage to keep several jobs going at once. Individual construction workers can earn up to two hundred yuan a month, four or five times the salary of the average factory worker in a state-run enterprise.

As we walked around the house, there was little doubt that the notion of building and possessing such a piece of private real estate was a very compelling one for my friend. He pointed out with loving care the marble slabs and wooden doors he had salvaged from the Minzu Hotel, in downtown Peking, when it was being remodelled. With pride he took me over to an antique window he had had framed into one of the house's stucco walls. And as we strolled around this nearly finished private pleasure-dome, he confided his dream of someday turning it into a lakeside restaurant to serve the carriage trade from the rapidly expanding foreign community in Peking.

By the summer of 1984, the New China News Agency reported that more than 260,000 peasants from Hebei province alone were working on private construction jobs in Peking and Tientsin. Moreover, it encouraged this new influx of peasants into the building trades because it would accelerate "the pace of rural and urban construction, and boost peasant income by providing an outlet for surplus labor in the countryside.

Because of such home-building, all over China, the price of building materials began to skyrocket, with a serious inflationary impact on large capital construction projects, which suddenly had to compete with rural builders for scarce supplies of steel, concrete, wood, and brick. Some peasants have been doing so well under the new system that they have started taking vacations to various scenic spots around China. The *Economic Daily*, a financial newspaper published in Peking, reported that in 1979 a hundred peasants from the Shanghai area went on an unprecedented group tour of Hangzhou, a lakeside resort in neighboring Zhejiang province. In the first quarter of 1983, there were six thousand such tourists, and their number was expected to exceed fifteen thousand by the end of the year. One peasant from Hongqiao commune, near Shanghai, was quoted as saying that on his next vacation he wanted to have "a taste of travelling on an air-conditioned bus." And in July, 1984, the *Worker's Daily* reported that a group of fifty wealthy peasants were about to embark on a three-and-a-half-month vacation tour of Japan at their own expense—the first tour of its kind in China. Soon one began reading reports in the Chinese press about peasant entrepreneurs who had set up travel services to aid their prosperous comrades in making business and leisure travel arrangements.

What the Chinese leadership had formerly decried as *dangan feng*, or "the wind of wanting to go it alone"—the tendency of some peasants, in the nineteen-fifties, to resist collectivization—has now been officially approved. The Dazhai brigade, once the supreme model of collectivity, now has been labelled an "ultra-left experience"—an announcement that sent peasants all over China scrambling to blot out the slogan that read IN AGRICULTURE LEARN FROM DAZHAI. Almost all the old slogans have had to be cashiered. Billboards covered with exhortations to make permanent revolution and engage in endless class struggle were painted over with such blandishments as MAINTAIN HEALTH BY WASHING ALL FRUITS AND VEGETABLES and TAKE CAUTION IN CROSSING THE STREET.

In documents issued after the meeting of the Third Plenum, the Party declared that "all forms of responsibility systems" should be given support as long as they helped increase the production of goods and contributed to raising incomes. "There should be no restriction to particular forms, and no practice of arbitrary uniformity," the Party maintained, thereby giving peasants carte blanche to experiment with a variety of ways to "get rich by working." Although there was great diversity in the manner and degree to which different collectives had responded to the new policy, the Chinese were claiming, by May of 1982, that 98 per cent of all production teams had switched to some form of the responsibility system. They further claimed that between 1979 and 1982 the total value of China's agricultural output had increased by 7.5 per cent annually—more than twice the average annual rise during the previous twenty-six years—and that between 1978 and 1982 the annual income of the average peasant had more than doubled, rising to 270 yuan. At the end of 1983, the State Statistics Bureau announced that peasant annual income had again risen, this time by 15 per cent, to 310 yuan, and that this rise had spurred an almost 30 per cent increase in rural retail sales.

Government officials tirelessly extolled what they called "commodity production" and "specialized households," extended families that had set themselves up as small independent businesses buying and selling livestock, making handicrafts, engaging in transportation, doing construction work, or running small factories. So successful were these "specialized households" that by mid-1984, many had taken on the appearance of latter-day kulaks (well-to-do Russian peasants, who had a major role in reviving the failing Russian economy during Lenin's dalliance with capitalism under his New Economic Policy in the nineteen-twenties, but who were finally destroyed by Stalin in his later collectivization of Russian agriculture). What the future of China's "kulaks" will ultimately be is hard to say. But for the moment at least they are riding high, accumulating a degree of wealth that the Chinese countryside has rarely experienced in the past and representing a productive force on which the Chinese government is apparently becoming more and more reliant.

On the surface, the new policy seemed successful. But behind the public statements and the official statistics lay a more complex reality. While the responsibility system had stimulated a surge in over-all agricultural production, it also set loose forces that may in time prove to be much more significant. One ominous development concerns grain, which Mao called the "key link" in the Chinese economy. Between 1977 and 1981, the gross value of China's agricultural output moved dramatically upward for every commodity except grain. The average annual increase in the value of oilseed production was 26.2 per cent, of cotton 9.7 per cent, of sugar 15.6 per cent, and of meat 12.9 per cent. The average annual increase in the value of grain production, however, was only 3.5 per cent. The reason was that the government controlled the price, in order to keep the cost of this basic foodstuff within the means of the average city worker. The government sells grain to city workers for only a fraction of what it pays for it. If the government were to allow the price to float on the free market (which would undoubtedly stimulate production), it would have to greatly increase workers' salaries, thereby generating a spiral of inflation.

In short, the government needs all the inexpensive grain it can coax out of the peasantry. But since grain must be sold to the government at fixed prices, rather than on the free market like other crops, it is the least profitable for peasants, and they don't want to raise any more than their quota requires. Having filled their quotas, many peasants eagerly turn the rest of their land over to cash crops like vegetables, peanuts, cotton, and tobacco. The freedom that the responsibility system has given the peasantry is causing more and more land to be taken out of grain production. The area planted to grain in China has decreased every year since 1979. Although the government claims that grain production rose 11 per cent in 1982 and 9.2 percent in 1983, and was up again for 1984 as of August, some economists doubt the accuracy of these figures, and they further point out that if acreage planted to grain continues to shrink, rising yields will soon be cancelled and production will be lower.

Not only are some peasants refusing to grow more grain than they must to meet their quotas but many of them are leaving the land entirely, in order to engage in more profitable occupations. In fertile areas, this exodus has not created a problem, but in marginal areas, like certain parts of Hebei province, travellers have reported seeing land lying fallow for the first time in memory. Richard Gordon, an American filmmaker who has been in Shanxi province on and off over the past two years making a series of documentaries on village life, describes the flight of peasants brought on by the new economic policies as something like a brain drain. "Everyone knows that if he wants to get rich he's got to lease his fields and hustle," Gordon told me. "The result is that, at least in some rural areas, those who stay on the land and work under the hot sun for one yuan a day while others are making five times that amount or more in various other ways are looked down on as stupid." By the beginning of 1984, one-tenth of the rural work force of 32 million farm workers—made "redundant" by the responsibility system—were reported by the *Economic Daily* to have been absorbed by township industries.

However, not every peasant who abandons the land to seek his fortune strikes it rich. In fact, in some areas large numbers of peasants who have left their old collectives are now unemployed. Recently, the *Beijing Review* reported that in certain rural provinces, such as Zhejiang, roughly half the work force had become "surplus labor." Nonetheless, hardly a day goes by that one doesn't see articles in Chinese newspapers about clever peasants who have found a way to prosper under the new economic system. Na Debao and Na Deren, two brothers in Heilongjiang province, were reported, in the *China Daily*, to have made an extra five thousand yuan in 1982 by trapping rats in their village and feeding them to a colony of ermines they were raising for fur. Another item in the *China Daily*, headlined FROGS PROTECTED, reported that Hubei provincial authorities had been forced to ban the hunting and selling of frogs in order to protect them from extinction at the hands of profit-seeking peasants, who were selling frog meat in Wuhan—the provincial capital—for as much as five yuan per kilogram.

"Tons of frog meat have been pouring into the city from the countryside each day," the news item said. And a man in Anhui province was widely celebrated in the press for setting up a successful business to market his special brand of salted watermelon seeds (*guazi*), which he had named Xiazi Guazi, or "Idiot Watermelon Seeds." This was a far cry from the nineteen-sixties, for instance, when such entrepreneurs were officially accused of "speculating and wrecking markets, amassing large profits, and living parasitic lives," and when those who strove for higher wages were denounced as being contaminated by "the evil wind of economism."

In another new development, all over China but particularly in the south, small private factories have begun to spring up. One such factory, which I visited in Daqiang district (formerly Daqiang commune) in Taishan county, Guangdong province, makes photographically etched aluminum faceplates for electrical appliances. Owned and operated by a local man whose overseas Chinese relatives had put up the capital, the factory, situated off the main road in a small rural village, employed forty laborers on a piecework basis. It was only one of three hundred such small-scale private enterprises in the district, and judging by the residence of its owner, a three-story brick mansion with balconies towering over the rice paddies, the factory was doing quite well. Indeed, travelling in such provinces as Guangdong and Fujian, one saw more and more of these new multi-storied residences rising incongruously above the rural landscape. Many even owned telephones, one of the most prestigious hallmarks of China's new rural bourgeoisie.

Since it is no longer illegal in China to own private vehicles, many peasants are buying small trucks and tractors. In February, 1984, the *Yancheng Evening News* reported that during a two-week period after the Party Central Committee had issued a circular with the assurance that "the diversify-to-get-rich rural policy will last at least fifteen years," peasants in one suburb of Canton bought forty-six trucks for their private businesses. By the end of 1983 it was common practice for state banks, which until 1980 had had nothing whatsoever to do with any kind of private enterprise, to make loans for the purchase of such vehicles directly to individual peasants. In the four rural counties around Chongqing in Sichuan province, for instance, the State Administration Bureau for Industry and Commerce reported that by March, 1984, peasants had bought more than 2,760 hand tractors and 431 private trucks, and that nearly 2 per cent of the over-all provincial population was engaged in private commodity transport and distribution.

With the creation of millions of independent farms, the need to bring crops to market has made the transportation business very profitable. "If you have a tractor now in the countryside, it's worth its weight in gold," a student at Peking University told me. "Using a tractor to haul crops is one of the best ways for a peasant to get rich, because there is so much demand, and because diesel oil, which tractors run on, is subsidized by the government. And guess what! The private fellows are running circles around the state-owned transport companies, because they are more flexible, more efficient, *and* cheaper."

When I was in Canton in January, 1984, I rode in my first private taxi, an ancient Shanghai-brand sedan that rattled and wheezed down the street; it had been bought from a state enterprise by two young unemployed men with a loan from "an acquaintance." Peking saw its first private peasant-run taxi company—with ten cars—take to the roads in June, 1984.

In April of 1984, a surprising photograph appeared on the front page of the *Beijing Daily*. The photograph showed a smiling Chinese family of six, the father with baby in arms, posing proudly beside a brand-new, shiny Toyota. The caption read: "A lady travelling far . . . Sun Guiying, a Peking chicken farmer, this week became the first peasant in China to own a car. She is pictured with her family beside the silver

Toyota for which she paid 9,300 ¥. Last year Sun purchased a five-ton truck for 21,000 ¥ to develop her business based in Dongerqi village in Changping county. She and her family have this year already sold 32,000 kilograms of eggs at a profit of 37,000 ¥ [about $18,500 U.S.]. Sun plans to use her Toyota to develop contacts and promote sales." Sun is a new model worker, one of the growing number of Chinese owning private vehicles. In fact, by the end of 1983, *Beijing Review* reported that 2.12 million peasants privately owned hand tractors (a 110 per cent increase over the previous year) and 89,000 privately owned trucks (a 523 per cent increase).

In rural Guangdong I discovered that small private ferry-boats had begun operating at many river crossings that had once been served only by state-run boats. I also learned that small private buses had begun to operate on certain routes in competition with state-run transit. By and large, such private transport vehicles are limited to short local runs, while the larger state-owned transport enterprises continue to monopolize the intercounty and interprovince routes. But in March, 1984, the State Council issued a new set of rules permitting private firms or individuals to compete directly with the state even on crosscountry runs. The New China News Agency described the decision as "a breakaway from the traditional government monopoly of transport," and "the latest step to encourage the development of rural commodity production." Such inroads of private ownership did not stop with land and water. In April, 1984, the New China News Agency reported that Guo Yuanying, a "well-off peasant" who lived in the suburbs of Zhengzhou in Henan province, had become the first Chinese peasant ever to buy an aircraft, in this case a Chinese-made Bee-3 light plane worth 19,500 yuan. Guo was reported to have plans to set up a fertilizer- and pesticide-spraying operation to serve local farmers.

Apparently, though, not everyone in China was pleased with this explosion of free enterprise in rural transport. At least some officials were resistant to the idea of private entrepreneurs competing with state-owned transport companies. Early in 1983, for instance, several trucks and tractors purchased by a group of peasants in Hunan province were confiscated by local officials, who accused the group of "encouraging capitalism." Eventually, this incident became something of a *cause célèbre* and caught the attention of Party officials in Peking. An article appeared in the *People's Daily* headed IS IT RIGHT TO CONFISCATE PEASANTS' TRUCKS AND TRACTORS?—a question to which the *People's Daily* replied with an unequivocal no, saying that such enterprises were "conducive to activating commodity production in the rural areas, and therefore should not be limited so long as they are not associated with speculations or other illegal activities." A companion commentary in the paper described the confiscation of the vehicles as "exploitation in a disguised form," which was "counter to Party policies and state law." In the end, the exploiting officials evidently saw the error of their ways, and returned the expropriated vehicles to their owners.

In March, 1984, the *People's Daily* reported another, similar case involving seven peasants in Zhengyang county, Hebei province, who had banded together to set up a private vinegar and soy-sauce factory. After applying for and receiving a license from the county's commercial bureau, they built their factory and commenced production. But less than a month later, a leader of their local commune had their license revoked on the grounds that the commune already had such a factory, which would only suffer from the competition. According to the *People's Daily*, the seven peasants decided to protest and sent a telegram to the provincial party secretary, who immediately ordered that their business license be reinstated. The *People's Daily* applauded this action in a front-page commentary and stated: "The Party's policy is to back the peasantry so that they may prosper through hard work. This is part of our over-all policy aimed at the prosperity of the entire nation."

When the *People's Daily* runs articles like these, the intention is not simply to rectify a single wrong but to send a political message all across China. In these cases, the message was clearly going out to all unreconstructed Maoists to get with the spirit of the responsibility system and the new Deng Xiaoping line, or else. It is hard to know how many of China's forty million Party members share the political sentiments of these Maoist officials. But at least a third of the Party joined between 1966 and 1976, the years of the Cultural Revolution, when the main criterion for membership was a commitment to radical Maoist ideology. Presumably, many of these Party members still hold such political convictions and view recent developments in China with abhorrence.

Certainly one clue is the way controversial cases like the confiscated trucks or the revoked license for the vinegar and soy-sauce factory keep popping up, each report in the press assumedly being, in essence, another case of local resistance to the present Party line—and representing no one knows how many unreconstructed Maoists or supporters of other forbidden tendencies just awaiting their moment to re-emerge. Certainly such cases, when publicized by the Party, have consequences that in the long run may be double-edged for the Party itself. For in each instance the Party is forced to put itself on record in the anomalous position of taking the side of the agent of free rather than collective enterprise (a record that everyone is aware will hardly be forgotten should there be a future shift in power at the center). One recent case in Zhejiang province, where the manager of a very successful privately owned shirt factory came under fire from local leftists, produced this—for China—amazingly bald headline in the *China Daily*: PARTY BACKS BOLD MANAGER ACCUSED OF GOING CAPITALIST. It takes little imagination to realize the possible consequences for the journalist who wrote that piece and his editor, not to speak of the central authorities who supported that line, should some form of Maoism again become ascendant in a future China—or to realize how high the stakes are for everybody involved in China's currently shifting political line.

When one set of leaders and one political line are in the ascendancy in China, it is very difficult to estimate the strength of the opposition, since they control none of the organs of propaganda. However, one can get a sense of that strength by reading between the lines in the Party press. For instance, if the *People's Daily* is constantly trumpeting the "correctness" of a given policy, how firmly "resolved" the Party is to carry it out, and how the masses are not being "deterred" from supporting it, one can safely assume that the articles have been provoked by opposition some-where. Further evidence that not all Chinese are pleased with what they have seen of Deng Xiaoping's style of mod-ernization is the "rectification campaign," launched in the fall of 1983. According to Central Committee documents issued in October, the aim of the campaign is to eliminate "serious impurities of thought, style, and organization" within the Party, to end "weakness and flabbiness," and to "consolidate the Party" by helping those comrades who still believe in the Maoist incarnation of the Chinese Revolution to "correct their mistakes" and throw off "the shackles of past leftist ideas." That some Chinese are still not in step with the new line was evident when, a month later, the municipal police force of Wuhan drove some five hundred private retailers from the city's main street, claiming that they were in violation of traffic regulations. Perhaps mindful of the rectification campaign, Wuhan's mayor, Wu Guan-zheng, later apologized to the displaced entrepreneurs, prom-ised them that they would be compensated, and treated them to lunch. So widespread did such conflicts become that, in July of 1984, Hong Kong's Communist newspaper, *Ta Kung Pao*, noted that readers might have "the impression that the left is staging a comeback." That same month, the Party issued a nationwide circular calling for the "complete and final elimination of leftist influence" from its membership.

One aspect of the new economic system which surely must rankle those whose minds are still filled with "serious impurities" and "leftist ideas" is the increasingly common practice of the hiring of labor by private businesses. Theoretically, of course, Communists are absolutely opposed to the idea of exploiting labor for profit. "The state's adoption of a flexible economic policy does not mean giving a green light to the revival of capitalism," He Jianzhang, the vice-director of the Institute of Economics of the State Planning Commission, and Zhang Wenmin, an assistant research fellow at the Chinese Academy of Social Sciences, wrote in *China's Economic Reforms*, an anthology recently published by the University of Pennsylvania Press. "True, China's Constitution allows the existence of an individual economy, but one which does not exploit others. Permitting the hiring of hands . . . runs counter to the basic principles of scientific socialism. When China proposes to let some people get rich first, this means they will do so not by exploiting other people's labor, but by adhering to socialist principles."

Nonetheless, the hiring of labor, particularly at small, collectively owned factories, is rampant. What is official government policy? No one I talked to in China seemed to have a clear idea of it. One Chinese thought that a limit had been set at eight employees. Another said seven. Someone else had heard that private businessmen could hire apprentices but were otherwise limited to drawing their work force from their families—although he admitted with a laugh that this would be an absurd regulation in those villages where almost the entire population had the same surname.

Like so many other things in China, government policy on the private hiring of labor is in a state of flux. But although there are no set rules, the practice is not actually unregulated. Most Chinese have a keen sense of what they can get away with, even without knowing the formal limitations of the law. Particularly now, when the promulgation of regulations lags so far behind the changing situation that rules are often obsolete before they are printed, people must operate with an almost extrasensory awareness of what is "permissible." They are highly sensitive to the unwritten rules that form quite real boundaries around their lives.

It was not until I happened upon an October, 1982, clipping from the *New York Times* that I was able to put the question of labor for hire in Deng's China into perspective. In the article, by the *Times'* Peking bureau chief, Christopher Wren, a personage described as "a leading comrade of the Central Committee" (I assumed him to be General Secretary Hu Yaobang) was quoted as saying that although "we should not encourage this practice [private hiring], this does not necessarily mean that we will use administrative orders to stop it."

A little over a year later, while discussing new economic policies with Liang Ying, chief of the foreign affairs office in Taishan county, I asked him what sort of limitations there were on hiring private labor in his area. He looked at me with a smile and said proudly, "You can hire as many people as you like. There is no limit." Wondering if the era of limits had ended for private investment as well, I asked him if there were any guidelines restricting the amount of private capital one could invest in a private business. "There is no limit for this either," replied Liang Ying unabashedly. "You can invest as much private capital as you want, and your private factory is permitted to get as big as it can."

★

William Hinton first visited China in 1937. He returned ten years later, with the United Nations Relief and Rehabilitation Administration. After the Communists came to power, he stayed on—as a tractor technician and a teacher—until 1953, when he went back to the United States to write a book and to run a farm of his own, in Pennsylvania. In 1966, he published *Fanshen*, an account of land reform during the late nineteen-forties in the Shanxi village of Long Bow

(Zhangzhuang). A later book, *Shenfan*, published in 1983, documents the subsequent process of collectivization in the same village.

When I ran into Hinton, a tall, solidly built man with a shock of white hair, in Peking, he was just back from Inner Mongolia—where he had been serving as an agricultural consultant at a demonstration center in Wengniute county run by the Ministry of Agriculture and Forestry and the United Nations' Food and Agriculture Organization—and was about to leave that night for a visit to Long Bow. "Frankly, I'm not sure they know where the hell they're going," Hinton said when I asked him about his views on how the responsibility system was working in the Chinese countryside. "The government is claiming great success with agricultural production, but some of the things I have been seeing leave me feeling a little less optimistic. In Mongolia, where the economy is basically pastoral, most sheep and cattle used to be owned communally, but now they've been divided up and contracted out to private households. The people get to keep all the wool, milk, and meat for three years, and after that they have to pay the collective back, with animals of equivalent worth. So everyone is on his own, and, of, course, people are all trying to make as much money as quickly as they can, by breeding all the animals they can get their hands on to increase their herd size. The result has been severe overgrazing. Everywhere you go in Mongolia, people tell you that twenty years ago the grass was up to the bellies of their horses. Now much of the land has been turned into dunes by those incredible Mongolian winds, which can scoop up a foot of topsoil that isn't anchored with grass and blow it into the Sea of Japan, a thousand miles away. In the spring, the wind can blow for three days running, at eighty miles an hour. The air becomes so full of dust that you can't go outside."

Local authorities in Mongolia are not unaware of the problems that Hinton described. In fact, a few days before I spoke to him a radio station in Inner Mongolia had broadcast an urgent appeal for all "units and individuals . . . to vigorously plant grass and trees . . . to rescue the grasslands from degenerating and becoming sandy deserts." When I asked Hinton if state efforts to regulate the use of Mongolian grasslands under the responsibility system had been effective, he replied, "Not as far as I can see. They have a lot of plans, but basically everyone is just doing his thing and looking after himself. There was a state-run grass-seed farm, for instance, up next to our demonstration center. It was an important operation, in my view, because it was one of the few places growing seed to replant badly overgrazed pasture. Well, the order came down from Peking to get the thing working on the responsibility system, which meant that the seed farm would no longer receive a government subsidy and would have to survive on its own profits. The manager was smart enough to know that there was no profit to be had in raising grass seed. So what did he do? He divided the whole place up into small plots and rented them to farmers to raise cash crops. Out of about three hundred and thirty acres of land, only eight remained in grass-seed production. The manager got himself a profitable bottom line, but meanwhile Mongolia is blowing away. And you see this same kind of problem all over the country. In Central China, private herdsmen are grazing livestock on mountainsides that should be left alone or they'll end up in the Yellow River."

Environmental consciousness has never been particularly strong in modern China. People have been more concerned with simply making it through each year than with planning for the long term. In the last few years, however, as China has quieted down politically and has been increasingly exposed to the outside world, some Chinese scientists have become attuned to environmental concerns. Articles on environmental issues are beginning to appear; one ran in the *People's Daily* while I was in Peking, headed STRENGTHENING LAND CONTROL IS A TASK THAT BROOKS NO DELAY. The author noted that "in some places . . . land resources have not been reasonably used and have instead been seriously undermined, resulting in loss of fertility, soil erosion, desertification, pollution, and degraded ecology," and concluded that "land waste and destruction have become a major hidden peril in China's rural areas."

"Of course there are *some* worried officials," Hinton said, with a sigh. "But what can they do? The privatization of everything has obliterated whatever collective consciousness there was about problems like land use. The leadership in the communes and the brigades, which could have been effective in dealing with these long-term problems, has been weakened, leaving the farmers to push everything to the limit in their own blind self-interest."

Richard Gordon, who was working on a film in Long Bow, also expressed concern about the weakening of the leadership of the collectives in the countryside. "I think it's true that most peasants are glad to have the Party off their backs," he told me. "But there are some really critical aspects of agriculture—like the maintenance of terrace walls, or flood control, or dams and irrigation projects—which just can't be taken care of by individual households. How is the government going to organize large numbers of people to deal with these problems, now that everyone is farming separately? For instance, there's a reservoir near Long Bow, built during the Great Leap Forward, from which water used to be pumped to the surrounding land. But under the responsibility system problems arose. The people who pumped water into the canals would do their work only if they were paid for the amount of water that left the pumping station. Long Bow, however, wanted to pay only for the water it received, since it usually got only about a third of the water that left the station; the rest leaked away, evaporated, or was stolen by villages closer to the reservoir. There was a stalemate, and, with no water being pumped, peasants began stealing the concrete blocks that lined the canals and using them to build houses. They ripped out all the copper wiring from the motors in the auxiliary pumping stations along the canals and sold it as scrap. The irrigation system has been destroyed, and since there is no longer any collective organization, there is no one to rebuild it."

When I returned from China, I talked about these problems with Wang Guangsen, a professor from Northwest Agricultural College, near the city of Xi'an, who in 1983–84 was a visiting scholar at the Food Research Institute of Stanford University. "The mobilization of masses of people in the nineteen-fifties did accomplish a good deal, although sometimes the projects were poorly designed and inefficiently built," Professor Wang said. "The amount of irrigated land in China increased by a hundred per cent. In fact, I myself worked on some of those projects."

I asked him how people would be mobilized now.

"Well, it will no longer be as easy as it was," Wang admitted. "We can no longer just force people to do things. A peasant's income used to come from the collective. If he didn't participate in collective labor, he didn't get paid. But now—well, I am somewhat concerned. We must find a new way. We must persuade the peasantry that in the long run such labor is in their interest. The Party and the government must do more ideological work."

Behind such fears lies a more menacing scenario suggested by the rise and fall of past dynasties during China's long history. The foundation of Chinese agriculture has always been the communally constructed waterworks that provided irrigation, the network of canals that facilitated inland transport of grain, and the elaborate system of dikes that contained China's rivers during the floods that periodically ravaged the land. One measure of every dynasty's success was how well it maintained this basic infrastructure. Failure to do so often contributed to massive peasant rebellions, which swept one ruling dynasty after another from power, leaving its successor to rebuild the failed waterworks through the corvée (forced labor) or suffer a similar fate. When Mao's Communist revolutionary movement came to power in 1949 after years of war, like any dynasty it, too, turned its attention to the waterworks upon which the salvation of China depended. As Profesor Wang had pointed out, it accomplished a great deal, even though the technological level of the country was extremely low. What will happen twenty or thirty years from now if, under the present Party policies stressing short-term gain, attention to the system of hydraulic works proves insufficient is a subject few Chinese today are willing to contemplate.

It is tempting, now that the Party has thrown its full weight against the communization of China, to write off the collective experience as an unmitigated failure. But this would be a distortion of fact. In many areas of China, Maoist collectivization was not a debacle. Analysts of China's economy generally agree that collectivization worked well in about a third of China's communes, had mixed results in a third, and was a disaster in the last third. But the Party appears to be paying little attention to the diversity of the country and the variety of experiences with collectivization, and, ignoring its own slogan admonishing cadres to "seek truth from facts," has moved to implement an across-the-board decollectivization.

"There is a powerful bureaucratic totalism in China even now, which makes it very difficult for any cadre to allow an exception to what he thinks is the general line," Richard Gordon commented after his sojourn in the Shanxi countryside. "Once the word comes down from the top, that's it. All the cadres feel obliged to jump on the bandwagon, no exceptions allowed. No one wants to make a decision that will expose him to criticism. This was true during the Gang of Four, and it's true now. The bureaucratic mentality is still just wicked." Professor Wang observed that "going to extremes is one of our problems." And William Hinton said, not without some exasperation in his voice, "The Party seems to be making no distinction between what is worth keeping from the old system and what is not. We are witnessing the breakdown of collective agriculture in China and the abandonment of an ethic that stressed working together rather than competing."

One vital service that communes and brigades provided in rural areas under the old system was what the Chinese refer to as the *wubao*, or "Five Guarantees": food, clothing, medical care, housing, and burial expenses for elderly, indigent, or sick people with no family resources of their own. But now that these rural organizations are being dismantled or reconstituted, it is unclear who is going to take over their welfare function. (The communes have become *qu*, or "districts"; the work brigades have become *xiang*, or "towns"; and the production teams have become *cun*, or "villages.") The press sometimes runs articles praising a county government for organizing "help-the-poor groups," or individual wealthy peasant families for voluntarily assisting poor neighbors. But what such articles suggest is that the government has no comprehensive welfare policy. "I don't think there is anyone looking after these people in an organized way now," William Hinton told me. "But what I am more concerned about is who is going to take care of people if there are floods, droughts, or famines, or if the rural economy suddenly goes sour. If any of these things happen—which is not impossible—there are going to be a lot of people back out on the roads begging, with no place to go and nothing to eat." He paused, and then remarked, somewhat fatalistically, "If you ask me, a situation like that would put China back pretty close to the way it was before 1949."

Although the situation today is far from what it was in prerevolutionary China, one is nonetheless beginning to see an increase in beggars, vagrants, and dispossessed children who roam the streets soliciting handouts. This suggests that, at least for some people, the welfare system has failed.

In Canton, for instance, I saw beggars in the streets, and indigents sleeping in doorways in the middle of winter. In fact, so widespread has Guangdong's reputation as a rich province become throughout the rest of China that poor people, or "civilized beggars," have begun to flood southward from Henan, Hunan, Jiangxi, and Anhui provinces in the hope of finding better living conditions. In Taishan county, I saw several pairs of small children begging. Signs explaining their plight hung from their necks. One little girl, who looked about eight years old and was roaming the streets with her five-year-old brother in tow, wore a sign that read: "Dear Aunts and Uncles: Our mother and father have died, and there is no one left to take care of us. Please give us some money and some rice coupons to help us live and have a lucky New Year." When I pressed a five-yuan note into the hand of the little girl, she looked at it and then exclaimed to her small brother, "Ahhhh! Fifty cents!" evidently unable to imagine that anyone would give her as much as five yuan.

Calling for greater efforts to help those peasants who were not sharing in the new wealth, the Rural Policy Research Center, the Secretariat of the Chinese Communist Party, and the Ministry of Civil Affairs issued a joint circular on March 18, 1984, urging that more local "help-the-poor groups" be formed, funds raised, and preferential treatment given to poor families in assigning land contracts and granting loans. But whether this kind of voluntary charity would prove an effective response to a problem that was likely to become increasingly severe seemed highly problematic to me.

Not only had the dissolution of the various levels of agricultural collectives removed one of the most effective safety nets from beneath China's poor peasantry, but it had destroyed the whole fabric of collectivized medicine, which had been one of Communist China's most successful institutions. Between 1949 and 1981, average life expectancy had increased from thirty-five to sixty-eight years, while the rate of infant mortality had dropped from 250 to 40 deaths per thousand. In large measure these impressive achievements had been brought about by China's decentralized but highly organized system of public health built around the now defunct communes and work brigades. Not only was preventive medicine stressed at the lowest level by paramedical "barefoot doctors" but each peasant was entitled to inexpensive cooperative medical care financed by his or her collective work unit. But as William C. Hsiao from the Harvard School of Public Health pointed out in an April 5, 1984 report in the *New England Journal of Medicine* entitled the "Transformation of Health Care In China," this old system is quickly becoming a thing of the past.

"As a result of economic reform," Hsiao wrote, "collective financing and popular support for the cooperative medical system have diminished. The proportion of the rural population protected by this system has been reduced by 50 per cent. In 1979, it was estimated that 80 to 90 per cent of the Chinese rural population was covered by an organized cooperative medical system. According to senior public-health officials, the latest survey shows that only 40 to 45 per cent of the rural population has such coverage."

Hinton and Gordon had both observed another growing problem in the countryside: a form of "decollectivization" not sanctioned by the authorities. "In the rural areas, people are ripping apart and dividing up everything they can get their hands on," Hinton told me. "They figure that if things are being parcelled out they had better get in there and get their share before someone else does." Gordon recalled how peasants in one village "decollectivized" a school. One peasant took a door, another took a few beams, and a third left with the windows. "The theory seemed to be that since the school was owned by all of the people, and since an order had come down to decollectivize, people ought to divide up schools just like land," he said.

When I discussed the incident with Professor Wang, he replied softly and with concern, "Yes. Some small factories, even schools and clinics, have been destroyed during the process of instituting the responsibility system. We worry about this sort of thing. We want the peasants to improve their lives by making use of the collective means of production as well as the private. But sometimes people get carried away. It's quite serious, but it cannot be helped. Perhaps all we can say is that compared with the beneficial effects of the responsibility system, all these matters seem relatively small."

Another communal resource that has been decollectivized in this manner is heavy farm equipment. Visitors to the countryside have seen earth-moving equipment and large harvesting machines rusting on the ground, stripped of all their salable spare parts. "Actually, most of those big machines are white elephants now anyway," Hinton remarked during our conversation. "Since fields have been divided up again into small plots, there is no way the peasants can use elaborate farm machinery. In fact, it's hard for most farmers to justify any kind of mechanized equipment. Except for small grain-grinding machines and transport vehicles, there is now virtually no agricultural mechanization. It may have been the first of China's Four Modernizations, but, as far as I can see, it is dead in the water."

The Four Modernizations—agriculture, industry, science, and national defense—are the foremost preoccupation of Deng Xiaoping's new program. William Hinton is not the only one who has expressed skepticism about the Four Modernizations. The Chinese themselves, who adore satirizing the various lists of numbered dos and don'ts (the Three Exterminations, the Four Clarifications, the Five Dare-Nots) that government propaganda organs put out, have facetiously concocted their own version of the Four Modernizations: the elite-ization of the cadres; the freedom-ization of the peasantry; the bonus-ization of the workers; the diploma-ization of the intellectuals.

Occasionally the official press will acknowledge the apprehensions felt by such Chinese. On January 27, 1984, for instance, the *People's Daily* admitted: "Among comrades holding leading posts, there are quite a few who are wavering, and among production-brigade and production-team cadres, many people who do not endorse taking production down to the level of the household." Their rationale: "The responsibility system damages the superiority of socialist collective management, letting it slide in the direction of individually managed, divided fields and individual farming that runs counter to the direction of socialized large production." Moreover, the article continued, these cadres fear that the new reforms will lead to "individualist ideology," "expand the difference between rich and poor," and allow "thirty years of extremely hard work to vanish overnight, returning [China] to a pre-liberation situation."

Of the official Four Modernizations, agricultural mechanization appears to be the one that has suffered most. Over the past few years, many factories that made farm machinery, with the notable exception of those plants that make hand tractors, which could be used in transport on the road, have either gone out of business or have been forced to retool in order to manufacture more profitable items. Melinda Liu, a correspondent for *Newsweek*, told me about a farm-machinery factory in Shandong province which retooled to turn out tinfoil for cigarette packages. Jack Potter described a visit to a tractor-repair station in Guangdong which had begun making household furniture. At the same time, the demand for donkeys and other kinds of draft animals has risen dramatically in the countryside, and so has their price. Xinjiang, China's westernmost province, has been shipping donkeys to Central China by the hundreds of thousands and making a tidy profit. (Some wags refer to this process as the "donkey-ization" of China.) Chinese officials, when they refer to agricultural mechanization at all these days, speak of it somewhat defensively. It is still enshrined as a long-term official goal, but except for some vague ideas about groups of peasants getting together in the future to buy expensive machinery and certain kinds of very small scale implements that are popular, no one seems to know how agricultural mechanization can be carried out on a large scale, given the realities of farming under the responsibility system. Inquiries about its fate are usually met with a barrage of official statistics demonstrating how spectacular production has been, as if the question of farm machinery were irrelevant to the future of Chinese agriculture.

Rather than reinvesting in agriculture, the Chinese appear to be relying on the existing infrastructure. The question is whether they will continue to show gains in production if they do not reinvest, bringing in new technology or efficiencies of scale. But decollectivization has in effect left such matters in the hands of the peasants themselves. A peasant who farms land under a three-year contract might be willing to buy fertilizer and better seed strains, but he would be understandably wary about investing his capital in long-term projects with no immediate payoff, like field terraces or irrigation. If he had any excess capital, it would be much more prudent, from his perspective, to invest it in a profitable sideline industry or to buy a truck and go into the transportation business.

Paul Pickowicz, the chairman of the Chinese-studies program at the University of California at San Diego, has made a number of visits over the past five years to the Wugung commune, in Hebei province. Over lunch at the Peking Hotel, he spoke of the future of peasant investment in Chinese agriculture as "an unanswered question in my mind," noting that agriculture is now in competition with sideline industries for private capital. "In Wugung, it is the burlap, ropemaking, cotton-spinning, poultry, and mink-raising industries that are really giving households an infusion of money," he told me. "Everyone knows that if you are interested in big money you don't invest in agriculture."

To try to remedy this problem and create a greater feeling of long-term responsibility for the land these peasants have contracted to farm, in February of 1984, the Party issued "Central Committee Document No. 1," which urged local units to consider granting longer leases—fifteen years or more—as the second generation of responsibility contracts begins to come up for renewal. However, such a step is far more awesomely fraught with potential dangers for all concerned than, say, the Party's defense of private capital in the more urban areas; for it raises, however covertly, the question of *de facto* ownership and inheritance, which it was believed the Party had laid to rest forever in the nineteen-fifties, when all buying, renting, and inheriting of land in the countryside was abolished.

Many peasants have already begun treating their contract land as if it were their own. Some, who had contracted for land but then found more lucrative ways to make money in commerce, have begun renting their fields to others, often collecting handsome amounts of money under the table from neighboring farmers who wish to expand their own agricultural operations.

The government has evinced a certain ambiguousness about this trend. On the one hand, they applaud the ways in which larger holdings have promoted more efficient production; on the other hand, they are disturbed by the way peasants have begun to wheel and deal with property still technically owned by the state. In fact, a May, 1984 report issued by the Land Management Bureau under the Ministry of Agriculture, Animal Husbandry, and Fishery expressed alarm at the way land had begun to be treated as a proprietary commodity under the responsibility system. "Illegal land-dealing has become a national problem," admitted Ma Kewei, vice-director of the bureau, who went on to cite numerous cases where collectively owned land had been illegally bought, sold, rented, and traded by state enterprises as well as individuals in contravention of the Chinese Constitution, which states explicitly: "No unit or individual is allowed to infringe upon, buy or sell, lease, or illegally transfer land."

In 1975, an official with whom I was working in the Dazhai brigade proudly told a group of us the following joke: "One day before liberation, peasant Wang was preparing to return home from work in the fields. Before he picked up his things to leave, Wang decided he would reassure himself about the extent of his holdings by counting his five tiny plots of land.

But no matter how carefully he looked and counted, he could tally only four of them. Try as he might, he couldn't find the fifth. When it was almost dark and he was ready to give up, he picked up his cap, and there, at last, under his cap, he found the fifth plot."

Peasant plots in the old China were so small and scattered that they were not only hard to find but hard to farm efficiently and harder to guard from thieves during harvest time. When land was collectivized and farmed communally, these problems became much less pronounced. Crop theft, in particular, was easier to control, because the members of the collective could take turns protecting the common fields from poachers. With the land once more divided up into a patchwork of small plots, the burden of guarding crops has again fallen on each individual household.

Commenting on his experiences in Shanxi, Richard Gordon told me, "All over the countryside, you see little guard shacks in the fields, where peasants now have to spend the night watching their crops. Not only do they have to work all day farming but they have to stay up all night as well. And by the time harvest season approaches, you can feel the tension in the air. As soon as one family starts gathering its crops, everyone else in the area is forced to begin also. It's like a wind that sweeps across the land. No peasant wants to be the only one with crops still out in the field, because he knows he is just setting himself up to be robbed." William Hinton noted the same phenomenon. "In some places, peasants have started harvesting way before their crops are ready, because of thieves," he said. "Sometimes they will cut three weeks off the growing season, which means that they lose a good percentage of their crop by not allowing it to ripen."

Peasants who have contracted to manage orchards, fish ponds, livestock operations, and tree farms have also begun to experience problems with theft. The construction boom in peasant housing has created a big demand for lumber, which now makes tree farming a very profitable business.

Many of the trees are planted alongside roadways, where they do not take up precious land and are easy to harvest; but since they are spread over miles of roads, they are also difficult to guard. At night, poachers will sneak out, saw down a few trees, and haul them away before daylight. Hinton told me that thieves have even been sawing down telephone poles. "It's not as if there were just a few isolated people out there stealing," he said. "There are organized gangs of young toughs roaming around And if there are enough of them they don't care whether something is guarded or not, as long as they can overpower the guard and get what they want."

"I think what's happening is that the countryside is beginning to divide up, particularly among young people," Gordon observed. "There are those who have already started to succeed and get a stake in the new system. And then there are those who haven't succeeded in getting anything, and are beginning to realize that they probably never will. They are the kind of people who join gangs."

Chinese travellers have also reported that along public highways local toughs, and even some corrupt officials, have begun to erect toll stations to extort money from passers-by, creating a situation reminiscent of the warlord era in the 1920s. "Some people feel that there is a kind of growing anarchy in the countryside, which makes the government fearful lest they lose control," a representative of the Chase Manhattan Bank told me in her office in the Peking Hotel. "On the other hand, however, they seem to have decided that the only way to liberate energy and get the kinds of rural production levels they want is to give up some of this control. The whole thing is such a contradiction. I don't know what kind of a system we have here, and I don't think the Chinese do either."

"My estimation is that what is going on right now out in the Chinese countryside is momentous," Charles Freeman, a diplomat who was deputy chief of mission at the United States Embassy in Peking, told me one day in his office.

"Looking at the way China's ideological affinities have changed over the last few years, I think you'd have to say they represent a sharper shift than in any other country since the U.S. occupation of Japan and Germany after World War II. All the old questions about what China represents are being reanswered. They are trying to modernize and still maintain some sense of their old identity. But unfortunately, they don't have a new doctrine to explain everything that's happening. The result is that because all these policies are still evolving, no one is really clear about anything."

"The truth is that I don't think Deng Xiaoping has any great vision like Mao about how Chinese society should be," David Bonavia, the *Times* of London correspondent in China, told me in Hong Kong. "I think he feels that grand visions of ideal societies are premature for China right now. What he sees is that his people are poor and his country is backward. And he is a very practical man. What he really wants is for his country just to produce, and I don't think he really cares how or what the short-term social repercussions are. One might say the Chinese are pretty much meandering across a new landscape in the fog."

★

Before the new economic policies were put into effect, commercial enterprises did their buying and selling through official government purchasing agents, called *caigouyuan*. But with the decollectivization of agriculture and the decentralization of industry, individuals and enterprises alike have begun to transact business directly with each other, in an environment that is increasingly competitive and market-oriented. This new universe of deal-making between buyers and sellers has engendered a subclass of people called *touji shangfan*, or "speculating brokers," whose function is to serve as middlemen by arranging deals, for which they get a commission.

A *caigouyuan* assigned to a factory in Hunan province, for example, used to be able to buy coal from Shanxi mines through government channels at a fixed price. Now the factory must make its own arrangements for coal, by sending a middleman to the mines to negotiate with—and wine, dine, and even bribe—mine officials until an acceptable deal is concluded. The Chinese call this process *yanjiu yanjiu*—a fortuitous double-entendre meaning "to make a study of a situation" and "wine and cigarettes." (When I asked William Hinton about the current status of *yanjiu yanjiu*, he laughed and said, "In some areas, they're way beyond cigarettes and wine. They want girls and cash.") Out in the countryside, middlemen, although they operate on a much less grandiose scale, are nonetheless powerful. They may help a peasant market his produce, find a job for someone, locate a needed tool or spare part, or facilitate a deal. A middleman's currency is his *guanxi*—that invisible web of connections through which so much of China's business is now transacted. In some parts of China, middlemen have moved in and begun to control whole areas of commerce, so that if a person wants to start selling certain kinds of goods or engage in transport on a certain route, he has to pay what is in effect protection money.

Wang Dacheng, the economic editor of the *Beijing Review*, anticipating possible criticism in the minds of the magazine's foreign readers about the creation of new social substrata like gangs, wealthy peasants, and middlemen, wrote recently: "Some foreign friends lack understanding of China's current agricultural policy of a contracted responsibility system . . . [and] they wonder whether the system will lead to a class polarization." Replying somewhat defensively to his own question, he continued: "It is true that the maximum and minimum income gap among today's peasants is larger than before, and for a time in the future that trend will remain unchanged. But the income gap will not lead to class polarization, because public ownership of the means of production . . . still dominates the means of production. . . . This is fundamentally different from class polarization in societies dominated by private ownership."

But whatever the explanations official spokespeople like Wang offer, out there in the real world Chinese society is beginning to restructure itself around the exigencies of the responsibility system. New kinds of wealth and power are threatening to delaminate the "classless" society of Mao's era. It would be extreme to say that we can see the elements of a new middle class, or (as in the case of the unemployed young people who join gangs) of a new, disenfranchised underclass. But the potential is there, and it is hard to believe that the rapid redistribution of economic power will not eventually transform Chinese society in a radical way. Already, the once supreme power of Party cadres in rural China has been undermined. Perhaps the clearest evidence of this is the change in the work situation of such cadres. Whereas under the Gang of Four they were awarded "work points" for their political activities on behalf of the Party, now many have been told to "stand aside" politically, and, like other peasants, farm or get involved in some other kind of business to make a living.

"Money and the people who are making it have in large measure replaced the Party as a source of legitimacy," the American diplomat Charles Freeman told me. "This is a profound change, which I think has caused a weakening of Party spirit and power. The leadership has unleashed some very powerful and unpredictable forces. I think they imagine that the private and state-owned economic sectors can run parallel, something like the economic models adopted by Hungary and Rumania. But actually, China has gone way beyond these countries. What the ultimate effect of all this on Party power will be, I don't know. But the Chinese have a saying: 'When a bird gets too big, it breaks its cage.' "

Party power, particularly in the countryside, has always been an extremely difficult thing to assess. But one attribute of the Party which is not so elusive is its prestige. And, official statements to the contrary, it is clear that Party prestige in both the cities and the countryside is now at a low ebb. The reversals in the Party line, no matter how welcome, have helped further to dispel the aura of infallibility the Party has always striven to maintain, so that Chinese speak of the "Three Crises of Belief" (in the Party, in socialism, and in the cadres). But perhaps the most important change in regard to the Party is that the Chinese now have an alternative path to success: namely, wealth, which in bypassing politics also bypasses the Party. The Chinese are thus able to take their Communist Party and the whole political process a lot less seriously.

These days, few well-educated Chinese youths aggressively seek Party membership. The ones who do are more often than not inspired by self-interest rather than idealism, for the Party can still confer numerous privileges, such as faster promotions, better housing, educational opportunities, use of a car, and chances for travel. (In a resolution passed by the Central Committee at its second plenary session, in October, 1983, Chinese leaders themselves admitted their concern about growing mercenary tendencies within the Party: "At present, some Party members and Party cadres have completely forgotten that the Party's aim is to serve the people wholeheartedly. Instead of correctly using the authority and the opportunities given to them by the Party and the people to work for the well-being of the masses, they seek benefits for themselves, or for a handful of people close to them, in every possible way. . . . These unhealthy tendencies and degenerate phenomena . . . have severely damaged the image of the Party in the minds of the people.") Even armed with its perks, however, the Party often finds itself in the anomalous position of trying to persuade young people who have gained prominence on their own—athletes, movie stars, students who have been admitted to distinguished universities—to become members. Instead of being able to bestow prestige on its chosen, the Party has been reduced to recruiting members who can bestow prestige on it.

★

All the new problems that have arisen under the responsibility system are, however, dwarfed in significance by one: the rising population. Between the years 1964 and 1982, the population of China increased by 310 million people. Currently, twenty-five babies are born there each minute of the day. If this trend continues, there will be no way for China to raise its standard of living. Every increase in food production will simply be consumed by new mouths. These unsettling truths have goaded the Chinese government into instituting a policy of "one couple, one child," in the hope of preventing the country's population, numbered at 1.008 billion in 1982, from exceeding 1.2 billion people by the year 2000. Families who limit themselves to one child are granted bonus payments, higher pensions, and preferential treatment in housing and schooling. Families who have more than one child risk pay cuts, reduction in medical care, and assessments with special taxes. Women are required to report their monthly periods to health officials, so that conception can be detected early. Pregnant women who have not sought permission to bear a child, or who already have a child, are strongly urged—and very often forced—to have abortions, sometimes as late as the second trimester.

In cities, where crowding is particularly acute, and where government propaganda campaigns and control are most effective, the "one couple, one child" campaign has been quite successful. But nearly 80 per cent of China's population lives in the countryside, where, in the words of the *People's Daily*, the birth-control policy "will win or fail." The results in the countryside have not been encouraging. The Chinese government cites two reasons: "backward ideology" and "economic interests." "Backward ideology" refers to the Confucian aspiration of peasants to have large families, with at least one son to carry on the family name. "Economic interests" is a term that officials leave vague, because to be more explicit would be to acknowledge one of the most contradictory and deleterious aspects of the responsibility system: namely, the pressure it has put on peasant households to rear as large a family work force as possible. When rural life was collectivized, the backward ideology of the peasants was easier to overcome. Party cadres still wielded absolute power; moreover, the need to have a large number of children as a source of labor was obviated by the fact that people were farming together on collective land, making the size of individual families irrelevant. But now, with most rural households on their own, large families have suddenly become an economic necessity; recently, many peasants have begun to take their children out of school, in order to increase the labor power in their fields.

Even if a peasant and his wife conscientiously decide to abide by the government's birth-control policy, they may lose their resolve if their first child is female. Although it costs as much to raise a girl as it does a boy, and although birth-control officials count one child as one child regardless of its sex, peasants are convinced that a female child will not be as much help in the fields as a male child, and know that when a daughter comes of age she will marry and go off to live in the household of her husband. A peasant who has no sons not only will be left shorthanded in his fields but will have no one to take care of him and his wife in their old age, and no honor.

One traditional solution to this problem before the Revolution was infanticide. Now, under pressure from both the birth-control program and the realities of the responsibility system, peasants are once again killing their girl babies. In November, 1982, the *China Youth News* stated: "Some of the unfortunate children are left by the roadside or abandoned on street corners, while others are even drowned. Such cruel, inhuman, and brutal actions cannot be tolerated. . . . If this phenomenon is not stopped quickly, then in twenty years a serious social problem may arise: namely, that a large number of men will not be able to find wives." The paper noted that in certain rural areas three out of every five surviving babies were male. Recent reports from travellers indicate that in some parts of China up to 80 per cent of the surviving infants are male.

In March, 1983, the *People's Daily* quoted a spokesperson for the Federation of Women's Associations: "the drowning and killing of girl infants and the maltreatment of mothers of infant girls ... have become a grave social problem. These phenomena are found not only in deserted mountain villages but also in cities; not only in the families of ordinary workers and peasants but also in the families of Party members and cadres."

In February of 1983, a group of women from Hexian county, Anhui province, wrote a desperate letter to the *People's Daily* which was printed under the headline WE ASK FOR A SECOND LIBERATION. None of these fifteen rural women had succeeded in giving birth to a son, although one had as many as nine daughters. Expressing an acute sense of shame at their failure, they wrote: "No one wants to be the mother of an excessive number of children, yet not one of the fifteen of us is ready to give up. Even if we must die, we would still strive to have a son, so that we might be able to hold up our heads.... Here where we live, a mother without a son suffers so much discrimination and cruelty that we feel it is worth risking our very lives to escape it." Documenting the ways they were discriminated against, these women called on the government "to adopt a law stipulating that whoever publicizes views favoring men over women, and whoever insults mothers who only have daughters, be punished by law, and that the law be posted in large characters on walls in rural areas so that it will be deeply imprinted in the hearts of the people, and so that the momentum it creates will be as great as that when we obtained our first liberation." All across China, I saw posters propagandizing against infanticide and against the abuse of women who gave birth to females. Some proclaimed MALE AND FEMALE

ARE EQUAL; others, THE BIRTH OF A DAUGHTER IS LIKE RE-
CEIVING A BLOSSOM, or THE LAW GUARANTEES RIGHTS TO
WOMEN AND CHILDREN WHICH MUST NOT BE VIOLATED.

Desperate to produce sons, many peasant women have turned to religion and are once again making pilgrimages to temples, sacrificing to the traditional gods and spirits that once were and evidently still are believed to control such phenomena. Others have turned to old-fashioned super-stitious practices, seeking the help of priests, sorcerers, wizards, witches, and mystics in the hope of giving birth to a boy.

That it is even possible for women like these to turn, with varying degrees of openness, to such an array of traditional semireligious practitioners is in itself arresting and certainly one of the most startling indicators of the regression of mores in rural China. Of course, it could hardly be said that religious and superstitious practices ever completely disappeared from the Chinese countryside, even at the height of the Cultural Revolution's temple-smashing, but certainly they were attenuated. Most peasants would not have dared publicly to seek help or solace in such "feudal" practices. Exactly what their resurgence means today is hard to say, but it is almost impossible to overlook evidence of their revival.

While leaving the campus of Xiamen (Amoy) University in the coastal province of Fujian on a winter day in 1984, I stopped at one of the privately owned shops near the front gate which sold candy, cigarettes, and fruit. As I was paying for a few oranges, I noticed that these small shops also stocked large quantities of incense and "gold paper," or fake wood-block-printed money, which Buddhist worshippers have traditionally burned as an offering to the gods. Since it seemed improbable that there could be much of a market for religious accouterments at one of China's most renowned universities, I asked the shopkeeper who bought these goods. Motioning behind her to the rugged, boulder-strewn mountain which divides Xiamen, and on which I had already noticed the sloping roofs of several buildings constructed in traditional Chinese temple style, she replied, "We sell them to the worshippers at Nanputo Temple over there."

Nanputo Temple is one of the most beautiful in China. Situated on the slope of Wulao mountain, it was dedicated in its present form to the Goddess of Mercy, Guanyin, by a Qing dynasty general after his reconquest, in 1683, of Taiwan, which lies only one hundred miles away across the straits from Xiamen. Closed during the Cultural Revolution, it was restored and reopened like so many other churches and temples after the fall of the Gang of Four and the ascendancy of Deng Xiaoping to power.

What I found striking about Nanputo on this visit was not only its physical beauty but the fact that so many Chinese, both young and old, came there to worship. They burned incense and left offerings of money to the Four Great Heavenly Kings (Si Da Jingang), whose large, imposing statues stand just inside the temple gate, and who are said in Buddhist mythology not only to hold up the four corners of the universe but also willingly to intervene in world affairs on behalf of mortals who were suffering an injustice. The worshippers bowed and said prayers before the image of Sakyamuni (Gautama Buddha) in a pavilion up a flight of stone steps from the gate. They lit incense and made offerings of fruit before the three-faced statue of Guanyin which resides in the uppermost part of the temple in the Hall of Great Compassion. Then, before leaving, many faithful also stopped to burn a few packets of "gold paper" in the small, tile-roofed brazier that stood to the side.

"What do people come here to pray for?" I asked one woman whom I had seen placing a bouquet of burning sticks of incense in front of Guanyin.

"Oh, the usual," she replied, not without a little embarrassment. After we had chatted for ten minutes or so, and she felt more comfortable, she said, "The men pray for wealth and long life. The women pray for a good marriage and to give birth to sons."

As we talked, three People's Liberation Army soldiers arrived at the temple. From their accents I could tell that they were from North China. They did not burn incense or "gold paper"; instead, they preoccupied themselves with taking photographs of one another like tourists. Still, it would be hard to express, to someone who had not actually witnessed PLA soldiers during the Revolution's purer Maoist phases in pre–Deng Xiaoping China, the shock of now seeing their benign and informal presence here at Nanputo. Watching them delight in their picture-taking, I was reminded that most PLA soldiers are in fact young peasants whose feelings, despite their khaki uniforms and hats affixed with a single red star, may hardly be different from those of the faithful burning incense at temples like this one. In being here, they are a living contradiction, a reminder that only recently China was a militantly Maoist society dedicated to the eradication of all signs of religion. They make one realize how amazing it is that Nanputo Temple should be here at all, with its fifty Buddhist monks in residence (ten ordained priests, forty novices) and a lay following from Xiamen of over a thousand people.

For the last two decades, the Chinese government had relentlessly tried to extirpate every sign of religion from society, proclaiming that there was no place in the Chinese Revolution for such feudal and useless superstitions. But now that China seems to have doubled back on itself in so many ways, religious worship is once again permissible, and temples and churches all over China are reopening.

Like their recent espousal of the capitalist ethic, the Party's rehabilitation of religion creates a contradiction between the past and the present which sometimes seems so enormous that it is hard to reconcile both periods as belonging to the history of the same country. Yet even now, after temples like Nanputo have been restored at great expense to the state and allowed to reopen, beneath the veneer of freedom of religion that the Chinese government today claims to guarantee its people, an ambivalence is evident. Proclamations of religious freedom notwithstanding, Chinese leaders continue to denounce religion.

This paradox was perfectly captured by Article 46 of the Chinese Constitution adopted by the Fifth National People's Congress in March, 1978, which read: "Citizens enjoy the freedom to believe in religion . . . to believe in atheism and to propagate atheism." Although the most recent Chinese Constitution, promulgated in 1982, makes no mention of atheism, an internal document issued by the Central Committee in 1981 declared: "We Communists are atheists. We must be unremitting in propagating atheism. . . . Our Party proclaims and implements a policy of freedom of religious belief, but of course, this does not mean that Party members can freely believe in religion. The policy of freedom of religious belief directed toward the citizens of our country is not applicable to Party members. . . . Any member who persists for long in going against this proscription would be told to leave the Party."

Just as the Chinese Communist Party wished to release the productive energies of free enterprise without becoming contaminated by the whole value system of capitalism, so it seemed to wish to be known by the world as a country that allowed religious freedom while at the same time trying to contain what it considered the undesirable side effects of unfettered religious life. And so, almost everywhere I looked in China, I saw the Chinese government trying to rein in the very religious forces its new policies had just emancipated.

In many respects, control of the Chinese Buddhist movement within China proper (overseen by the government-controlled Chinese Buddhist Association in Peking) presented the government with the least problems. Chinese Buddhism is essentially a nativist religion with few ties to the outside world. Moreover, it is a highly individual form of worship, not dependent on the kind of congregations that make other forms of religion more of an organized threat to the supremacy of the Party.

The Protestant churches, however, are not only quite different in their organization from the Buddhist Church but have traditionally had very close ties through Western missionaries, with parent church organizations abroad. Viewing them as much more of a threat than the Buddhist Church, the Chinese have compelled the over four hundred Protestant churches estimated to have reopened since 1979 to join the "Three Self Association," which pledges them to be "self-supporting, self-governing, and self-propagating" —namely, to be indelibly Chinese and maintain no official connection with any Western counterpart churches.

But government efforts to control these churches have not been as effective as some Party leaders might have wished. When religious activity was banned during the Cultural Revolution, millions of believers went underground to worship in what Chinese refer to as "home worship churches." After Protestant churches began opening their doors, in 1979, many worshippers once again began to attend officially approved services. But many, many others, having become accustomed to their "home worship," remained determined not to associate with state-controlled religious activities, and continued to hold illegal underground services. Some have since been arrested, causing their brethren to become even more alienated from the Chinese state and more defiant than ever in their opposition to its control over religion.

Chinese Catholics found themselves in an even more contrary position, left dangling somewhere between Rome and Peking by the new policies toward religious freedom. Although many Catholic churches have also been restored and reopened in China during the past five years, all have had to join the Catholic Patriotic Association, which since 1957 has maintained no relations with the Vatican and refuses to recognize any papal authority over Chinese Catholic laymen or clergy. The government's refusal to recognize the Vatican stems from its long-held view that the Pope has historically been an agent of imperialism in China, dominating the Chinese Catholic Church through his appointments (many of whom were not even Chinese) and interfering in the country's internal affairs. However, a lot of Chinese Catholics, particularly "home-worship" Christians, have simply refused to go along with the Patriotic Association, and continue to be loyal to the Holy See. Over the years, many have been arrested and languished in jail, sometimes for decades.

In recent years, the Pope has made several efforts to heal this rift. The papacy's close ties with Taiwan, however, have been a continuing point of contention. And the situation was not improved when, on February 22, 1982, the Pope called on Catholics worldwide to pray for those who were suffering "religious persecution" on the Chinese mainland. The Catholic Patriotic Association called the charge "malicious slander" and "an insult to God" as well as to the "independent, self-ruling, and self-propagating Catholic Church" in China.

The Pope's statement not only further inflamed relations between Peking and Rome but also reminded those Catholics who had been struggling against the Chinese government for years that their struggles were not going unnoticed. It appeared to make them more obdurate than ever, at the same time that it made the Chinese government more determined to crack down. Further arrests followed. In March of 1983, for instance, four Jesuit priests in Shanghai were tried for anti-state activities and sentenced to lengthy prison terms. In June of 1983, Francis Xaxier Zhu Shude, who had already spent years in prison during the Cultural Revolution, was again arrested for refusing to sever relations with the Vatican. After sixteen months of detention, he was sentenced to twelve years in prison for "colluding with foreign countries, endangering the sovereignty and security of the motherland, collecting intelligence reports, fabricating rumors, and carrying out incitement."

Of all organized religions in China, none has proved more difficult for the government to manage than Tibetan Buddhism, which during the long period of Tibetan resistance to Chinese occupation in the nineteen-fifties and nineteen-sixties came to be intimately associated with Tibetan nationalism. Politically charged as the religious situation is in Tibet, the Peking government has nonetheless allowed those few monasteries and temples that were not destroyed during the Cultural Revolution to reopen. But controls are far from lax. Religious life in all temples and monasteries in the Tibetan areas of China is carefully orchestrated by the Association of Tibetan Buddhists and the Chinese-controlled Religious Affairs Office. Even on matters of doctrine and ritual, these overseeing organizations have the final say.

For instance, the Tibetan Buddhist Association still forbids the ancient practice of replacing deceased "living Buddhas" (*tulku*) with the new incarnations of their enlightened souls. This practice traditionally involved elaborate searches throughout Tibet for a specific young child who would be invested after discovery by the officiating lamas as the successor and the new living Buddha. A search often involved astrological consultation, divinations, dream interpretation, and other magical practices the Chinese Communists consider irredeemably feudal and superstitious. But unless the Tibetan Buddhist Church is allowed to replenish its dwindling number of *tulku*, among whom the Dalai Lama is the most eminent, it will be deprived of one of its most important religious institutions and sources of leadership—which is, undoubtedly, the very point of the Chinese prohibition.

The Dalai Lama, who was himself a *tulku*, and both the spiritual and the temporal leader of all Tibetans, fled to India in 1959 before advancing Chinese troops, and has maintained a movement in exile opposed to the Chinese occupation of his country ever since. As he is Tibet's spiritual leader, it is quite natural for the Buddhist clergy inside Tibet to be drawn to him, but such manifestations of loyalty all too easily acquire political significance. During the fall of 1983 and the winter of 1984, the Chinese Public Security Bureau began making arrests of various religious figures who had advocated Tibetan independence or maintained contact with the Dalai Lama. In September, shortly after I left China on my first trip, reports reaching Peking claimed that the Chinese were scheduled to execute five Tibetans as part of the anti-crime campaign, including Geshe Lobsang Wangchuk, a lama from the Drepung Monastery in central Tibet, who had been responsible for writing wall posters against the Chinese occupation.

On October 3, the U.S. Tibet Committee, a group sympathetic to the Dalai Lama, claimed to have received information that some 1,500 arrests (including many political dissidents) had been made throughout Tibet, that four executions had been carried out, and that five more were scheduled. Amnesty International, believing these arrests to represent mass violations of human rights, cabled Chinese leaders in Peking in protest. Also in October, thirty-four other monks were reportedly arrested after being picked up at the site of the Ganden Monastery (destroyed during the Cultural Revolution by gangs of Red Guards with pickaxes and explosives), which they were endeavoring to rebuild.

Controlling the dissident movements within China's various organized religions may, however, prove nowhere near as troubling to the Chinese government in the long run as another similar but more chaotic development: the rapid return of popular religious cult practices and traditional superstitious beliefs to the countryside. Travelling around China in the early nineteen-eighties, one heard of them and saw evidence of them everywhere, almost as if they were sprouting like hardy weeds in fields left fallow by the withdrawal of the Party—or at least of its prestige and power. Traditionally, it has been from exactly such fertile ground that, in China's long history, all sorts of dissident and rebellious movements have sprung to life to challenge a weakened but still reigning dynasty.

In traditional Chinese peasant society, everything was

believed to be subject to the controlling power of the myriad gods, spirits, and immortals that populated the Buddhist and Taoist pantheons. From Confucianism, China's "state religion," the peasantry derived another important religious practice: ancestor worship, which called for honoring the dead lest the spirits of neglected ancestors work evil on the family and alter the harmonious relationships between present life and the hereafter.

Not only was this world of traditional belief and practice viewed by Communist revolutionaries as a useless drain of time and energy on the people, but it was also considered a tool of the ruling classes to keep the peasantry mired in superstition, backwardness, and ignorance. Upon coming to power, the Communist Party had striven with great vigor to expunge every remaining vestige of these old feudal systems of belief from rural life. But as I kept seeing and hearing about aspects of this traditional peasant religious life—which I had assumed to be long since rooted out by the seemingly inexhaustible revolutionary energy of Mao's followers—it became clear that the Communist Party had, in many important respects, allowed the battle against superstition to lapse.

In the past few years, numerous accounts of traditional peasant cult practices—previously a taboo subject—have appeared in the Chinese press. Travellers in China have also recounted witnessing or hearing about rituals and ceremonies that had not been thought present in China for many years. The press reported, for instance, that in Hebei province peasants were once again consulting geomancers before constructing buildings and graves; while Richard Gordon told me about peasants in Shanxi who had started to rebuild small shrines to local tutelary gods and spirits, and about officials (including some Party cadres) who had participated in elaborate rituals to make it rain.

Officials in Peking complained that peasants had begun refusing to have the bodies of dead relatives cremated, and instead were secretly burying them outside the city with the traditional ceremonies of burning paper money and possessions so that the deceased might have material ease and comfort in the afterlife. According to the *Peking Daily*, such practices had even been the cause of fifty-six forest fires in 1982 and 1983. A Chinese priest told me about a Catholic church outside Shanghai to which peasants had flocked from as far away as Shandong province in the North because of widely circulating rumors that the Virgin Mary would perform a miracle.

In Guangdong province, I myself saw rural households with protective paper gods pasted up on either side of the doorways and incense burning in front of newly installed ancestral altars. In one small market town, I saw peasants selling traditional paper gods such as Cai Shen the God of Wealth; Zhu Tudi, the Pig Earth God, who makes swine grow fat; and Songzi Niangniang, the Goddess of Childbirth. In Fujian province I was told about peasants who had taken up collections to rebuild village temples to propitiate local gods and spirits in hopes of a good harvest.

Such isolated bits of evidence are doubtless no more than the merest hints of what is actually going on. China, which recently seemed bereft of all aspects of traditional religious life, once again appears to be brimming over with belief in the bizarre and the supernatural. In fact, by allowing greater toleration of religion, the Chinese leadership has confronted itself with the almost impossible task of trying to differentiate between "religion," which has become acceptable (albeit to a limited degree), and "superstition," which is still forbidden, at least in a theoretical sense.

When Wen Fushan, vice-governor of the Fujian Provincial People's Government, was asked by a *Fujian Daily* reporter what the difference was between legitimate religion and superstition, he replied: "This is a good question. The main differences are: first, normal religious activities must be patriotic and law-abiding and must support the Communist leadership and the socialist system; second, they must have a legitimate organization that is recognized by the government departments concerned and accepts their leadership; third, they must . . . not affect production and the social order. But superstitious activities like witchcraft, sorcery, the use of elixirs, fortunetelling, astrological practices, invocations to avert calamity or make rain, supplications for offspring, treating disease with exorcism, the practice of physiognomy and geomancy, building village temples, and so forth do not have the special characteristics of modern religions, and thus violate the regulations stipulated by the law. . . ."

Wen concluded his interview by urging "the broad masses of people to study Marxism-Leninism–Mao Zedong Thought diligently, to study cultural and scientific knowledge, to guard against and relinquish the pernicious influence of superstition, and to dedicate themselves heart and soul to the Four Modernizations."

Evidently many Chinese did not find these distinctions quite so self-evident. As one writer in the *Guangming Daily* noted: "Many cadres still cannot distinguish between religion and feudal superstition. They think that anything involving the spirits and the gods is religion, so they incorrectly conclude that the policy of freedom of religious belief applies also to feudal superstition. The difference is that religion is a way of viewing the world, while feudal superstition is a means by which some people practice fraud."

By way of trying to discredit superstitious practices, Party-controlled magazines and newspapers began over the past few years to run more and more articles reporting on people who were harmed by such activities. One particularly gruesome tale, clearly meant to suggest the unfortunate end awaiting those who succumb to superstitious beliefs, was published in January, 1982, by *China Youth News*. It was the bizarre story of a woman, Wang Yuying, in Hebei province, who believed she was immortal, that pigs were fairies in disguise, and that her visions of green dragons were real. When an uncle with whom Wang had frequently fought died, she believed that his ghost had returned to haunt her and entered the body of her thirteen-year-old son. For a year she paid a sorcerer to come almost daily to exorcise the ghost. But convinced that the boy continued to be possessed, Wang and her husband, Chang Siyong, finally beat their son to death with a rolling pin. Two months later, in another story, *China Youth News* reported the drowning of four primary-school girls who believed that they could become immortal and ascend to heaven by walking across a certain reservoir.

In January, 1982, the *Guangming Daily* ran an item about a man named Zhang Delong, a member of Chencun commune in Hebei province's Nangong county, who came to believe that the gods had caused a brick to appear in his wife's stomach. In an effort to remove this supernatural brick and cure his wife of her stomach ailment, Zhang and his sister were reported to have tried to reach down her throat and pull it out with their bare hands. The woman ultimately died of suffocation.

In May, 1982, the newspaper *Ming Bao* carried a story about a Sichuan peasant, Shi Zhuqiang, a former barefoot doctor from Daxian prefecture, who had been sentenced to death for "making use of feudal superstition to carry out counter-revolutionary activities." Shi, claiming that he was the Jade Emperor, the main divinity of the Taoist triad and protector of the common people, had travelled to various villages in his area performing the ancient ceremony of "the emperor ascending the throne." Evidently many peasants (and even some Party cadres) actually believed Shi to be the mythological Jade Emperor, and went before him to make offerings. Some brought him food and money in the belief that he could "treat patients and eliminate misfortunes." Certain women were even said to have consented to perform sexual acts with him as offerings.

One night while Shi was performing his ritual in the Longtan commune, a woman with two infant daughters was reported to have come forward, fallen on her knees, and asked the help of the Jade Emperor. However, her two small children began to cry in fright, and Shi became enraged. Claiming that they were committing lèse-majesté, he called them "antimonarchist" and ordered them drowned in a nearby rice paddy. When the mother refused to relinquish the children, Shi himself grabbed a hoe and beat them to death. After first throwing the children's bodies into a night-soil pit, he ordered his followers to retrieve and burn them so that no evidence of the murders would remain.

On April 16, 1982, Jade Emperor Shi was executed.

The *Sichuan Daily* ran an equally horrific story about a peasant, Yin Xianfu, who was told by a witch that his family of seven had been "dispossessed of their souls by the god of heaven." On the witch's advice, Yin set fire to his house, in which his wife, son, daughter-in-law, two grandsons, and two granddaughters had just sat down to a ritual feast before their deaths. Although his family was killed and Yin was reported to have been burned when he tried to throw himself on the pyre, he survived. The whole way to the hospital he was said to bewail the fact that he had failed in his effort "to go to heaven."

In October, 1983, the *Chinese Peasant Daily* reported another bizarre incident in Sichuan, involving a "witch doctor" who had been paid one hundred dollars to perform an exorcism on a tubercular patient. While the family looked on, the witch doctor hit the patient several times on the head, claiming that the blows would release the evil spirit. The patient promptly died, at which point the witch doctor proceeded to cut off his genitals and head, promising that this would facilitate his immediate rebirth as a woman.

One of the most graphic examples of superstition conflicting with modernization was reported from Hainan Island in the south, where peasants, believing that oil exploration had angered the traditional wind and water spirits usually taken into account in geomancy, attacked an oil rig and destroyed $300,000 worth of oil-drilling equipment.

Such stories appeared frequently in the Chinese press,

and even taking into consideration the Party's self-interest in using them as negative lessons, they do suggest how profoundly peasant life has changed in China over the past few years. Whether a new floodtide of traditional religious practices will engulf China, whether young people will find them at all persuasive, and what effect they may have on the course of social and political development in the Chinese countryside is, of course, impossible for an American so far removed from the scene to say. However, their presence injects new and explosive contradictions—to use a term once popular in the Maoist lexicon—into Chinese society, ones that are all too familiar to students of China's history in the nineteenth and twentieth centuries. Just as on the economic front China was apparently trying to move forward by returning to an older, precommunist set of values, so its new policies with regard to religion harked back to an earlier time. While the new modicum of religious freedom was welcomed by many, in certain crucial ways it allowed for a resurgence of precisely the kinds of peasant superstition that Mao Zedong's generation had spent so much energy trying to destroy. At times it seemed as if the new Chinese leadership, without quite being willing to realize or admit it, was in the process of turning their revolution inside out.

★

"Small production engenders capitalism and the bourgeoisie continuously, daily, hourly, spontaneously and on a mass scale," Lenin, whose works are still accepted as the orthodox canon in China, wrote in 1920. Is China "going capitalist"?

Chinese Marxist theoreticians confidently maintain that as long as the state owns the major share of the means of production—that is, the land and the large industrial plants—no one need have any fear of incipient capitalism. "Clearly it is not a Marxist approach to make a universally applicable truth out of a statement Lenin made in

1920 in the context of the specific conditions in Russia,"
wrote Fang Sheng, an associate professor of economics at
Peking University, in a piece anthologized in *China's Economic Reforms.* "He was referring to a situation in which
the private economy was still predominant, and the question
of which would win out—socialism or capitalism—was still
at issue. Because some individual businessmen have impressive incomes, sometimes more than the average earnings of a worker in a big enterprise, people say, 'What else
could this be but capitalism?' This is a superficial prejudice.
Big incomes and fat wallets mean getting rich and nothing
more."

A Party official from Jiangxi province named Wang
Yuanlong reflected this thinking in an interview with a correspondent from the *Beijing Review.* "The gap between the
rich and poor at the moment is caused mainly by the difference in their ability to work," he said. "It is not a sign
of class polarization caused by exploitation. . . . We'll never
allow the emergence of two antagonistic classes in the countryside a second time. Our goal is prosperity for all. But
like people riding bicycles, not everyone can ride abreast
of one another. Our peasants, too, do not all become better
off at once. Some are better off earlier than others, [but]
we must not go back to egalitarianism, in which case no one
would be in a position to prosper."

In March of 1983, on the centenary of the death of Karl
Marx, General Secretary Hu Yaobang gave a long speech,
entitled "The Radiance of the Great Truth of Marxism
Lights Our Way Forward," which sounded as if it had come
out of a time warp. "From its very birth, Marxism has
demonstrated its mighty power, with which no ideological
system can compare," he proclaimed with a confidence that
seemed sublime. "We have learned from Marx, conscientiously studied and drawn wisdom and strength from his
works, and shall continue to do so. . . . The past century has
demonstrated again and again that the history of Marxism
is one of triumph over successive onslaughts by various

antagonistic ideological trends [and that] its revolutionary drive has remained invincible."

Hu's oratory notwithstanding, while I was in China I met no one who was drawing "wisdom and strength" from Marxism, much less moving forward under the light of its "radiance." I met few who gave more than the most perfunctory genuflection to Marxist ideology. What I saw and felt instead was the "radiance" of people making money. Behind the official façade of confidence what one sensed was a failing socialist nerve. Marxist true believers evinced a growing sense of their irrelevance to what is really new and vital about their country. Sometimes there was a tinge of humiliation in their polemics, as they stumbled and struggled to fit all the incongruities of the new situation into a convincing socialist framework. Like people whistling past a graveyard in the night, Chinese leaders were uncertainly feeling their way, and hoping that everything would work out all right. The Revolution's theoreticians have found themselves left with the hapless task of trying to provide ideological justifications for events that are beyond their control, and perhaps by now beyond the control even of the Central Committee itself. Nonetheless, Party propaganda departments continue to busy themselves with programs of mandatory instruction on Marxism for cadres, and with campaigns to promote "spiritual socialist civilization," which succeed only in creating a certain uneasiness about the political future and hardly disturb those who are busy getting rich.

Do any Chinese care that March has been officially declared Socialist Ethics and Courtesy Month? How many Chinese are stirred by the propaganda campaign to promote a list of socialist virtues, which include the Five Things to Stress (decorum, good manners, hygiene, discipline, and morals), the Four Things to Beautify (ideology, language, behavior, and the environment), and the Three Loves (for the motherland, for socialism, and for the Chinese Communist Party)? The last time China saw a moral crusade so disconnected from reality was in the nineteen-thirties, when Madame Chiang Kai-shek (Song Meiling) launched her "New Life Movement," a pastiche of Christianity and Confucianism designed to save China from the spiritual bankruptcy of communism.

When Chairman Mao finally came to power, he insisted that theory was indivisible from practice—a dictum that China's current leaders appear to have reversed, as evidenced in their seemingly Confucian belief that moral behavior can be cultivated apart from what is happening in the real world. Their efforts to instill socialist values in the Chinese people while at the same time encouraging them to lead lives that more and more resemble those of people in capitalist countries violate the Marxist notion that the superstructural world of values inevitably grows out of the substructural world of class and economic system. Like diplomats who stubbornly continue to represent their country abroad long after the government that appointed them has been deposed, the custodians of China's "spiritual socialist civilization" continue to preach the ethics of a system that is vanishing in front of them.

Some of the advocates of old-style socialist virtue are clearly Maoists battling against the new pragmatists with the only weapons they have at hand. But the conflict is within individual minds as well as between them. Many of China's leaders seem to have divided political personalities. Drawn in one direction by the Promethean spirit of free enterprise and individual initiative and by China's urgent need to modernize, they are drawn in the opposite direction by a yearning to maintain the integrity of China's Marxist revolution. And so they continue to extoll "socialist ethics" even while they release the forces of free enterprise, as if the spirit could somehow remain uncontaminated by the flesh.

But this reluctance to allow their old Communist ideology to slip away as the world changes under their feet is perhaps not so incomprehensible. After all, it was this very ideology that enabled the country to make its revolution in the first place and then to mobilize masses of people in the nineteen-fifties to build the agricultural infrastructure—large-scale irrigation, flood-control, and land-reclamation projects—upon which China still relies. Moreover, unlike most other Third World countries, where economic development is in itself a sufficient goal, China has always yearned for something more: to be a representation of some kind of greatness or spiritual infallibility. Mourning the failure of Confucianism—China's last great state orthodoxy—to save the dynastic system and the country at the turn of the century, traditional scholar-officials lamented that, with the passing of the old culture, China had lost what they called its *guocui,* or "national essence." And without that precious national essence, which had provided political balance and continuity with the past, China went reeling directionless into the first half of the twentieth century—one of the darkest periods of its history.

It was not until the advent of Mao Zedong and his revolutionary peasant nationalism that China was reunited and a new national essence began to crystallize, restoring Chinese pride and resolve. Now, like the old conservative scholars who clung with determination to Confucianism even as it was failing China, revolutionaries of Mao's generation hold on to the legacy of Marxism and Maoist thought even as they contemplate the evidence of its failure in their own policies. Perhaps they, too, are fearful that if China loses touch with this most recent incarnation of its *guocui* it will once more become culturally and politically deracinated, and will fall into ruin.

PART TWO

The
New
Open
Door

When I first arrived in Peking, in 1975, the skyline of the city was still dominated by traditional-style structures built during the Ming and Qing dynasties. The sloping roofs of the Temple of Heaven, the Front Gate of the old city wall, the pagoda on Coal Hill, and the towers, halls, palaces, and gates of the Imperial City provided the otherwise flat and drab city with at least a visible reminder of its ancient past.

Returning to Peking almost a decade later, I found the skyline transformed. All across the city, neighborhoods of old-fashioned *pingfang*, the tile-roofed single-story houses that had once composed Peking's network of residential *hutung*, or alleys, had been bulldozed. In their stead, square,

Western-style high-rise buildings now towered over the city, making the old landmarks seem suddenly smaller and strangely out of place.

One of the most recent additions to this new Peking skyline is the twenty-two-story, $75 million, 1,007-room Great Wall Hotel, whose three wings loom over the capital's eastern Chaoyang district like a misshapen grain silo on our own Midwestern prairie. At sunrise and sunset, its reflective-glass curtain walls shimmer in the orange light, accentuating the colorlessless of the other, low-lying buildings nearby. At night it fairly glows with electric light—an oasis of illumination in an otherwise dimly lit city where most people still have no more than a single bulb in each room, and public halls and stairways are usually left completely dark.

"The Great Wall of China [is] one of the most majestic monuments ever created. Today it has a notable rival, the Great Wall Hotel," reads a blurb in one of the hotel's brochures, entitled "Introducing China's Second Great Wall." At first, it seemed to me somewhat far-fetched to compare a hotel to the 1,500-mile structure started between 221 and 206 B.C. by China's First Emperor, Qin Shihuang, to keep out the "barbarian" tribes from the Mongolian steppes; but after living in the hotel, I must confess that its presence in the capital of the People's Republic of China seemed in many ways as extraordinary as the Great Wall itself, though with an opposite purpose—to draw the barbarians in.

The Great Wall is just one of scores of new Western-style hotels under construction, and a small part of the over-all effort being made by the Chinese government to lure foreign business and tourism to China with first-class Western-style tourist facilities, which now include such amenities as golf courses, theme parks, deluxe trains featuring opulent German-made sleeping cars and private dining coaches, hunting safaris to bag wild game such as boar, deer, bear, and lynx in the virgin forests of Manchuria (some of the few such areas remaining in China), luxury cruises, and expensive trekking and climbing expeditions into remote mountainous regions such as the Tibetan plateau or the Karakorum and Pamir mountains.

All these concessions to foreign wealth are the outcome of China's "open door"—a policy annunciated during the late nineteen-seventies—which in a few short years has transformed the whole chemistry of relations between socialist China and the outside capitalist world. The phrase "open door" was in itself a curious choice for a new foreign policy, laden as it was with historical overtones of an earlier, humiliating period of Chinese contact with the West. In 1899, United States Secretary of State John Hay, fearful that American businessmen would be squeezed out of China by Japanese and European attempts to establish semicolonial "spheres of influence," issued a series of diplomatic notes calling on all major powers to preserve the equality of trade in China. While Hay's "Open Door" notes did help assure the integrity of the Chinese government against the encroachment of imperialist powers seeking outright Chinese colonies, their initial impulse came more from American concern that our missionaries and businessmen not be excluded from China than from any outpouring of altruistic feeling. In this sense, the "Open Door" notes were not so much a call to the imperialist powers to moderate their aggressiveness as a way to insure that all powers would be able to exploit China equally.

To hark back today to an era when foreign imperialist powers were threatening to "slice up the Chinese melon," by recoining the phrase "open-door policy"* to describe China's new relationship to the West, makes one wonder

---

* It should be noted, however, that although the phrase "open door" is used by the Chinese government to refer *in English* to both American policy toward China at the turn of the century and China's policy toward the outside world today, the written Chinese for each policy is different. The former policy, in Chinese, is *menhu kaifang*, literally, "door open"; while the latter is *duiwai kaifang*, literally, "open to the outside."

about the Chinese leadership's sense of history. At the present moment, it seems hard to believe that Mao swept to power in the nineteen-forties in no small measure by addressing his revolution to the deep-seated feelings of humiliation, and even hatred, which the Chinese people had experienced as they helplessly watched their country fall prey to foreign exploitation, and that his first words upon entering Peking in 1949 were to proclaim that at last China had "stood up."

In fact, after nearly a decade's dalliance with the Soviet economic "model," and Russian advisers, Mao broke with the Soviet Union in the late nineteen-fifties and defiantly set China off on a course of its own, where self-sufficiency and a refusal to rely on the largesse or capital and technical expertise of any foreign power became ideological hallmarks of the Chinese Revolution. "Rely principally on your own strength, take outside help only as a back-up," Mao had admonished his people. With the capitalist West already historically seen as the imperialist opposition, and the Soviet Union viewed as a socialist betrayer, China set off to pull itself up by its own bootstraps. Succeed or fail, Mao's China seemed determined to do it on its own, beholden to no one.

All that has now changed in such a wholesale manner that few visitors who have seen China in both before and after phases can easily become reconciled to the contrast. Where once China's leaders eschewed foreign loans, foreign investment, and foreign managerial and technological assistance lest they become dependent on the wealthy industrialized nations of the imperialist West, under Deng Xiaoping's new "open door" policy they have begun to court them with an almost single-minded ardor. In a 1980 speech, for instance, Premier Zhao Ziyang admonished the Chinese, "We must not bind ourselves as silkworms do within cocoons"; other Chinese leaders no longer spoke exclusively of "self-reliance" but of "opening to the outside while invigorating the domestic economy" (*duiwai kaifang, duinei gao haojingji*).

On November 30, 1981, Zhao told the Fourth Session of

the Fifth National People's Congress: "In economic work, we must abandon once and for all the idea of self-sufficiency, which is a characteristic of the national economy. All ideas and actions based on keeping our door closed to the outside world and sticking to conventions are wrong. . . . By linking our country with the world market, expanding foreign trade, importing advanced technology, utilizing foreign capital, and entering into different forms of international economic and technological cooperation, we can use our strong points to make up for our weak points. . . ." On June 5, 1984, while visiting Belgium, Zhao confidently proclaimed: "China's door is open now, will be opened wider, and will never be closed again."

I arrived at the Great Wall Hotel on a bitterly cold Peking morning in January 1984. No sooner had my taxi pulled up beside the huge stone lions guarding the entrance to the hotel than two doormen trotted out and greeted me with a cheerful English chorus of "Good morning, sir. How are you today?" before ushering me from the car. Both wore neckties, black leather gloves, handsome fur hats displaying the seal of the Great Wall Hotel, and smart black uniforms with red piping around the jacket cuffs and down the sides of their neatly pressed trousers. Right behind them came two bellhops wearing crimson jackets with high mandarin collars. They smiled, also said "Good morning," and then moved efficiently to gather my things from the taxi's trunk and take them inside.

To someone who had not previously travelled in China, such amenities might have seemed natural enough, but in China, the revolutionary slogan of "serving the people" had never been translated into such service at hotels and restaurants, perhaps because it smacked of just the kind of exploitation Mao's revolution had set out to eradicate. So as those solicitious young men in their stylish new uniforms carried my duffel bags into the lobby, politely waiting for me to pass through the revolving door first, the disjuncture between the present moment and Mao Zedong's revolution against the "twin evils" of feudalism and imperialism seemed precipitate.

Once inside the hotel, which had opened its first few floors of rooms for business a month earlier, I found myself in an environment so different from any I had previously experienced in China that I felt as if I had crossed an unmarked international border into another country. From the lushly carpeted floor rose forty-foot-high columns encased in polished chromed steel. Kumquat trees were arranged for New Year's in artful clusters around settings of plush chairs and couches upholstered in purple. Unlike dry, cold Peking, the lobby felt as balmy and warm as the tropics.

"This hotel offers what no other can, a first-class international standard of service infused with the mystique of China," noted the Great Wall brochure. Actually the "mystique of China" seemed to have been quite effectively kept outside the hotel. What was most noticeable, in fact, was how successfully those responsible for designing the hotel had re-created an almost totally Western environment in the middle of a city that for years had resisted just such intrusions. As I waited for a reception clerk in a black three-piece suit and necktie to feed my name into a computer terminal at the front desk and issue me my room key, I couldn't help trying to imagine how a classical Chinese scholar might have felt upon arriving in New York City and being taken to the traditional Astor Court Chinese Garden, recently reconstructed to the last detail in the Metropolitan Museum of Art. It would all have seemed perfect, except the world from which it had been plucked would have been missing.

"Things have changed here in China," Lucy Hobgood-Brown, the American director of public relations and advertising for the Great Wall Hotel, told me two days later as we toured the hotel. "I don't really know how the Chinese decided to allow a hotel like this. But I do know that while I was working at the Dallas Hyatt Regency, they sent a delegation over to visit American hotels, and when they saw the Dallas Hyatt, they just fell in love with it. They adored the glass exterior and the atrium lobby from which you can watch the elevators go up and down! Originally they had only planned to come for an hour, but they ended up staying for three or four. They wanted to see everything. A year later we were told that they had decided to build a hotel in Peking based on the Dallas design."

Hobgood-Brown, who left her job in Dallas to come to Peking, is part of a fourteen-person managerial staff of foreigners that now runs the hotel. It includes general manager Peter Sun, a Chinese-American, two Swiss who serve as resident manager and executive housekeeper, two French who serve as food and beverage manager and executive chef, and eight Hong Kong Chinese from that colony's Mandarin Hotel. When I asked Hobgood-Brown whether she was enjoying her new job, she smiled broadly; then, pausing for a moment, as if not sure where to begin, she took a deep breath, sighed, laughed, and said, "This is the first time I've been involved in building something from the bottom up. I mean, the Chinese have just not had any experience running modern, first-class Western hotels. We all have our Chinese counterparts or 'shadows,' who are theoretically being trained to take over, but there's a lot for them to learn, and they are having to learn it very quickly, because we have President Reagan coming in April. As far as public relations go . . . well, at first the Chinese didn't understand the idea. They were used to running things like hotels without any promotion at all. They knew people would be forced to stay at what few hotels there were regardless of whether or not they were run well, because in the past there has been no competition and no alternatives. So, in trying to explain the whole concept of public relations to our Chinese counterparts, our general manager, Peter Sun, finally decided to just detail it all out very concretely. In the middle of his description, one Chinese jumped up and said, 'Oh! I get it! You mean propaganda!' " Brown laughed affectionately at the anecdote.

The Great Wall Hotel, the largest operating Sino-

American joint venture as of the beginning of 1984, was the brainchild of the Shanghai-born American businessman C. B. Sung, who joined his California-based Unison Pacific Corporation with the Becket Investment Corporation to form the E-S Pacific Development and Construction Company. As the new company's chairman, Sung raised the $75 million necessary to finance construction of the hotel from a consortium of Western banks led by the Nordic Bank of Scandinavia, and in 1979 signed a joint venture agreement with the China International Travel Service (CITS) to build the hotel, with his company holding a 49 per cent share and CITS holding a 51 per cent majority share in the venture.

Sung, who was educated in the United States at the Massachusetts Institute of Technology and Harvard University, was one of the first businessmen to pioneer U.S.-China trade after Deng Xiaoping's visit to the United States in January, 1979. He has not only brought the Great Wall Hotel into being but also helped facilitate a $51 million joint venture between the Jeep Division of American Motors and the Beijing Automotive Works to build four-wheel-drive vehicles in China, as well as investing in a third, smaller Sino-American joint venture, the Parker-Hubei Seal Corporation.

With China doing more and more business abroad and its tourist industry expanding by more than 28 per cent a year (more than 9.47 million visitors from 163 countries in 1983), China has been in desperate need of more hotel space. Sung's Great Wall Hotel was the second Western-financed and Western-run luxury hotel to open in the Chinese capital. In 1982, the 440-room, $22 million Jianguo (Build the Nation) Hotel, financed by the Chinese American architect and builder Clement Chen and run by the Hong Kong–based Peninsula Group (of the Peninsula Hotel fame), opened in Peking. In April of 1984, the Holiday Inn–Lido Hotel also opened, making it the first hotel on Chinese soil to be operated by a foreign chain, its rooms constructed as modules in Singapore and delivered as finished products to China. Numerous other joint-venture hotels were still under construction in other large cities, including China's first Hilton hotel in Shanghai.

Another very different kind of luxury inn, the 325-room, $25 million Fragrant Hills Hotel, opened outside the capital with much fanfare in 1982. Unlike the Western-style Lido, Jianguo, and Great Wall hotels, the Fragrant Hills was designed for the Chinese government by the Cantonese-born American architect I. M. Pei and included aspects of traditional Chinese design—such as a garden courtyard—in its conception. But what has proved so noticeably different about the Fragrant Hills Hotel is not just that its designer attempted a synthesis of Eastern and Western styles as a showcase for China's modernization efforts, but that it was completely state-owned, and when it opened it was entirely managed and run by Chinese.

When I visited the Fragrant Hills during the winter of 1984, I found it already beginning to look seedy, though it had been open less than two years. Walking through its glassed-in central atrium, and then through the four smaller wings that jut out from the four-story core building, I felt as if I were touring a museum that had been abandoned before being completed. Not only was there a depressing feeling of emptiness about the place—as if the hotel had never been properly moved into—but there were already stains and cracks in the walls, and broken furniture and fixtures that remained unrepaired. The bar was a bare, uninviting room with only one attendant in it, snoozing beside a small refrigerator that turned out to contain only a few bottles of beer. The shops off the lobby were barren affairs with few items of interest for sale. Pieces of trash blew through the gardens in the wind. I left the Fragrant Hills Hotel filled with sadness, and returned to the Great Wall without even having the meal I had originally planned on. I was reminded anew of how reliant on the outside world's pool of managerial skills and technology China's few pockets of modernization actually still were, and how difficult it still was to maintain any Western-style institution in the middle of China without foreign know-how and supply pipelines to the outside world.

With its foreign investors and management, the Great Wall Hotel is a universe apart from the Fragrant Hills: a world within a world that offers foreigners every service imaginable. For local Chinese, the scope of its imported luxury is unimaginable. It has a health club complete with gym, indoor swimming pool, sauna, steam bath, outdoor jogging track, and two competition tennis courts that can be floodlit at night. It is also the first hotel with an airline booking office in its lobby. For entertainment the hotel offers four lounges, including the Orchid Pavilion Court, where one can sit in a huge atrium tea garden in which glass elevators soar up the wall and—in the words of a hotel handout—"watch the world go by"; the Summit, an octagonal-shaped structure perched on top of the hotel like freezing coils on top of an ancient refrigerator, where one can "enjoy a breathtaking view . . . sink back in plush armchairs and relax as you sip your favorite cocktail . . . made just the way you like it"; the Caravan, a bar described as an ideal place "to enjoy a relaxing drink or a rendezvous"; and the Cosmos Club, a nightclub with "an atmosphere of electric intimacy, [where] midnight blacks blend magically with mirrors and chromes," where a guest can enjoy "contemporary live music from an imported seven-piece band until the early hours."

The hotel's Grand Ballroom can accommodate 1,800 people. When President Ronald Reagan visited China in April of 1984, he held a state banquet in the ballroom, where Chinese and American guests were served a meal of turkey flown in from the United States. (The hotel's Chinese chefs practiced on several preliminary turkeys in order to master this American culinary art before the presidential appearance.) When Reagan did arrive at dinner, a Chinese band played the national anthems of both countries. No words were sung, but if they had been, President Reagan would have heard the following collectively written lyrics:

March on, brave people of our nation.
Our Communist Party leads us on our new Long March.
Millions as one,
We march, we march on to the Communist goal.
Build our country,
Guard our country,
We will work and fight.
March on, march on, march on!
Forever and ever, raising Mao Zedong's banner, march on!
Raising Mao Zedong's banner, march on, march on, march on!

For the dining pleasure of its regular guests, the Great Wall Hotel offers four restaurants. Its flagship eatery, La France—described in a hotel handout as "certainly one of the finest restaurants in the Far East"—is overseen by full-time French chefs, including Roland Durand, winner of the coveted culinary award of *Meilleur Ouvrier de France*, and offers such gourmet specialties as *cornet de saumon fumé au caviare, terrine de viande truffée façon Escoffier*, and *noisettes d'agneau flambées aux trois moutardes*. When I visited La France, which had not yet opened, the Chinese staff was still being trained. One group was learning how to greet guests and take orders. Another was practicing carrying heavy trays around a slalom course of chairs. A third sat on the luxuriously carpeted floor listening to a lecture on French food.

Among the hotel's other restaurants, the Silk Road features a steak bar with imported meat, a luncheon buffet, and a Western breakfast. The Yuen Tai, a Sichuan restaurant on the twenty-second floor, offers the hotel's only Chinese culinary touch. In the Orient Express coffee shop, young waitresses in stunning American-designed blue, gray, and purple chemises serve European meals and snacks twenty-four hours a day. Unlike Chinese-run hotels, the Great Wall also offers round-the-clock room service.

The idea of being able to eat and play throughout the night, while the rest of China closes down and sleeps with an absoluteness hard for Westerners to imagine, was a disorienting one. Nothing like it has been seen here since the end of the old treaty ports. Before "liberation," in cities like Shanghai, Westerners could amuse themselves until early morning in their special clubs and night spots, and now, after thirty-five years of revolutionary upheaval, Western-style night life is once again making a beachhead in China's capital. Although today it is a phenomenon confined almost exclusively to foreign-run hotels like the Great Wall, I wondered how long it would be before Chinese too would demand to be part of the fun.

Night life is hardly the only new idea these Western hotels are pioneering in China. Telephones of the push-button variety produce not only room service and wake-up calls but also operators who take messages while guests are out, something Chinese-run hotels have never done before because of the language problem, and because the notion of such services has seemed so utterly alien here. The public rest rooms, which in most Chinese buildings are dark and dirty and smell of stale urine, are here spotless and nothing short of inviting. The floors of the whole hotel are covered with thousands of square feet of wall-to-wall carpeting, a concept of interior decoration which has no precedent in China, where people have traditionally treated hallways and lobbies as extensions of public streets, places to discard unwanted trash, put out cigarettes, drop gum, or spit.

Upstairs, the guest rooms, which range in price from $90 U.S. for a single to $800 for a luxury suite—three times the annual wage of the average Chinese factory worker—have wall-to-wall shag carpeting that still emits the unique smell of synthetic fiber, as exotic in China as it is familiar in the West. The beds have all been imported from the United States and are equipped with a console of buttons between the headboards, allowing guests to control the flow of air and the lighting, radio, and television like a pilot in the cockpit of a plane. In fact, almost everything in the hotel has been imported. The reflective plate-glass exterior came from Belgium, the bathroom fixtures from the United States, the carpets from New Zealand, the televisions and some of the room furniture from Japan, the lobby couches and chairs from France, the chandeliers from Italy, and much of the food from Hong Kong.

Like a space colony blasted into orbit bit by bit, the Great Wall Hotel was constructed out of millions of separate pieces imported from the outside world and then painstakingly assembled in China. Even after the building was finished, this reliance on the outside world did not stop. For most of its supplies, from copy-machine paper and dishwasher parts to coffee and steak, the hotel still must maintain a lifeline to that world beyond China's borders which its leaders were once so determined to do without. The surroundings were so familiarly American that I would awake in the morning fuzzy with sleep and not immediately remember what country I was in, even after I had looked around the room. Then I would draw the curtains that shrouded the double-glazed plate-glass window sealing my room from the dust storms of the cold Chinese winter, and there I would find Peking. Sometimes as I stood in my warm quiet room watching Chinese board buses or bicycle off to work, it seemed as if I were looking at nothing more than a television screen—an illusory image of China rather than China itself.

It is hard to emphasize strongly enough the conflicting sensations I felt while at the Great Wall Hotel. Being in a hotel so similar to others I had stayed in outside China, but this time in Peking rather than Dallas or San Francisco, was as strange an experience as any I had ever previously had here. Yet it was also clear that, like other developing enclaves of Western business and tourism now springing up all across the country, the Great Wall Hotel is providing a powerful new center of gravity in China, drawing to it not just accumulations of imported things but the developing dreams of both Westerners and at least some Chinese. Minimally, such enclaves are clearly designed to give foreign tourists and businessmen a way to be *in* China without being *of* it; to convey the feeling that everything is here within the confines of a single building, so that except for an occasional shopping spree, trip to a historical monument, or business meeting, there is no need to venture out. As Clement Chen, Jr., the California-based designer and 49 per cent owner of the Jianguo Hotel, told me, "Let's face it. We live in the twentieth century. People may enjoy visiting a country with an unfamiliar culture like China, but when they get back to their hotel from a tour in the afternoon, basically they want to be able to relax in a first-class place. What I mean to say is, after the Peking duck they may still feel a need for some bacon and eggs, a club sandwich, or maybe a steak. I purposely designed my hotel with these needs in mind, so that once a guest gets inside, he will be able to forget where he is and feel as if he were back home."

Being inside the Great Wall Hotel left me with that feeling of being in one of those Las Vegas casino hotels, where every whim of a guest is provided for so that he or she need never wander out the door away from the gaming tables. While I stayed in the Great Wall Hotel, I found myself so lulled by its convenience, efficiency, and capacity to provide for my every need, that leaving its comfortable embrace for the real world to see Chinese friends—which involved riding packed buses, eating in dirty, noisy, crowded restaurants, or attending entertainment events in Chinese theaters, which are invariably too hot or too cold—came to seem almost too difficult and unappealing to warrant the effort. Whereas in the past I had prided myself on always being as much as possible with Chinese friends as they went about their daily lives, I now began to feel like a parody of a journalist: the stereotypical reporter who gets his news from the English-language paper slipped under the door of his hotel room each morning, or from taxi drivers and elevator boys assigned to serve foreigners in their magnificent isolation.

What made this experience resonate was my awareness that from the time of their first significant appearance on the Chinese scene in the eighteenth century in Canton, and later in the treaty ports along the China coast, foreigners had always lived in isolation, whether by Chinese design or through their own wishes to maintain their Western style and standard of living. After the Communists came to power in 1949, they continued to isolate foreigners, although now for somewhat different reasons. The Party erected huge, graceless "guesthouses" in which foreigners could be cordoned off lest their bourgeois pollution rub off on the Chinese populace at large and contaminate the purity of the Chinese Revolution. In this sense, the Western-run Great Wall Hotel was only a luxurious polar twin of the older, drabber, Chinese-run hotels.

Even if today, after all the upheavals of recent years, the Chinese leadership still seems to be pursuing a strategy of isolating foreigners, by permitting these new, luxurious enclaves of containment, they are also inadvertently building great dynamos of foreign "pollution," beacons flashing exactly that message which earlier Chinese leaders struggled so hard to suppress.

One of my favorite pastimes in the Great Wall Hotel was simply to sit on the French couches in the lobby and watch; for just as the Great Wall bears no physical resemblance to Chinese-run hotels, so the lobby partakes of a completely different ambience. No uninviting void consecrated only to ingress and egress like the Friendship hotels of old or even I. M. Pei's Fragrant Hills Hotel, the Great Wall lobby invites one to linger and congregate. More important, it holds out the possibility of social encounter the way certain public squares and streets where people are fond of promenading do.

One afternoon I was watching Japanese, American, and European businessmen criss-cross the lobby in their regimental dark suits and ties, when through the revolving door came two older Chinese men wearing the kind of gray tunics and caps that Westerners have dubbed "Mao suits." Once inside the door, they paused, doffed their caps, and looked around in wonder. Almost all eyes turned to watch their uncertain entrance. Their tunics, which stood out so starkly in the Great Wall's lobby, made me recall that when China was still a messianic revolutionary society, Western pilgrims used to come by the thousands to see visionary socialism at work. So willing were they to embrace what they understood to be the Chinese Revolution that many eagerly donned such "Mao suits," in the hope, perhaps, that sartorial propinquity might help establish them in Chinese eyes as being on the right side of the capitalist/socialist divide. But as this ideological schism is dissolving before people's eyes, "Mao suits" have lost their symbolic power as representations of a new social force in the world. Rather than "revolutionary" they look simply "baggy," as many Westerners now describe them. Few visitors bother to wear them in a gesture of solidarity. In fact, more and more Chinese are themselves refusing to wear such clothes and are looking for exciting modern styles that will connect them symbolically, not to China and its socialist revolution of "workers, peasants, and soldiers," but to the new "revolution" that takes its inspiration from capitalism and the West.

At the moment of entry of these two men, who looked to be in their sixties and who wore so many layers of sweaters and long underwear beneath their tunics that their bodies had lost all human form, the feeling of the lobby was transformed. From being an isolated Western preserve, it suddenly became a confluence between two converging cultures, one living within the hotel and the other outside. I surmised that the two Chinese gentlemen must have arrived to meet a "foreign guest," since Chinese are rarely allowed to frequent hotels like the Great Wall unchaperoned, and in any event do not have the hard currency with which everything sold in them must be paid for.

After several minutes of gazing around like wild animals

that have just happened on the edge of an unfamiliar clearing, one whispered something to the other and gave him an encouraging tug on the cuff; then they both walked over and sat down tentatively on a couch opposite me, evidently uncertain about what to do next. Speaking Peking dialect with the most cultivated of accents, they finally began a conversation in soft tones, from which I gathered that they had come to the hotel to meet a Frenchman who was visiting China in some capacity or other.

"Has it been long since you ate with a knife and fork?" I heard one of them ask with an uncertain half-smile.

"Paris, 1948," replied the other with a self-effacing laugh, reciting the date the way a sommelier might announce the place and year of a vintage wine he was afraid had long ago spoiled.

Like so many other educated Chinese whose contact with the outside world was interrupted when the Communists came to power in 1949, these two aging gentlemen seemed overwhelmed and disoriented by their sudden resurfacing in cosmopolitan Western life here at the Great Wall Hotel, as if they were divers who had been brought up too suddenly from the deep. I left the lobby then, but about an hour later I saw the two men sitting in the Orient Express coffee shop with their French contact, a dapper man in cufflinks with a handkerchief blooming out of the breast pocket of his suit. I heard only a few snatches of French from one of the old gentlemen, and noticed that the other one, who had not used a knife and fork since 1948, had avoided embarrassment by ordering a sandwich. In that simple gesture I was reminded of how remote from all this the lives of most Chinese still were.

As perfect as was the physical plant of the Great Wall Hotel, there were, after all, still myriad ways in which the outside Chinese world sifted in. Although the hotel had installed modern pushbutton phones, which did facilitate easy room-to-room communication, a guest who tried to reach a Peking number outside would immediately run into the abyss of the Chinese telephone system. Sometimes one would have to dial numerous times before getting access to the outside, then, as often as not, the circuit would be busy, or the number itself would be busy, or one would be connected to the wrong party. One could easily be on the phone fifteen or twenty minutes to no effect other than tying up the wires. Frequently one had the sense that the entire city must be jammed in telephone gridlock with everyone on the phone but no one getting through. The touch-tone phones of the Great Wall notwithstanding, it was often more efficient and infinitely less frustrating just to take a cab or bus over to the office or residence of the person to whom one wished to talk.

There were as well more human ways in which the outside Chinese world registered inside the hotel. In the morning one could watch businessmen in the Orient Express eating breakfasts of croissants, poached kippers and lemon, steaks with hashed brown potatoes, or waffles with maple syrup. At first glance, one might imagine oneself to be at home; but looking more closely at the waitresses, it was not difficult to detect a note of tentativeness in the way they still went about serving foreigners Western food. Since most of them had been at work only for a month, they were not yet completely familiar with everything on the menu. Lucy Hobgood-Brown had told me that to avoid confusion, initially the chefs would cook one order of every item on the menu each day and set it out on a counter with the appropriate label so that the waitresses would not make mistakes.

Just as the Japanese tea ceremony is an elaborate ritual with carefully defined rules for serving, so in the West the morning rite of coffee drinking has its own imperatives. It was obvious at the Great Wall Hotel that the waitresses had not yet mastered these. For instance, they had not quite gotten the hang of cruising the floor with a coffee pot to freshen guests' cups before they drank their last few tepid gulps; and sometimes they would forget the cream, unaware that coffee without cream is as unimaginable for many Westerners as green tea *with* cream would be to the Chinese.

The clerks behind the front desk, in their dark three-piece suits and ties, were the spitting image of their Western-trained counterparts abroad, but if one observed them carefully, they too exhibited a hesitancy that would doubtless pass as they became more familiar with their new jobs. For now, though, when a guest approached to ask for a room key—which was kept in a numbered box on the back wall—the clerk would turn and have to hunt for it painstakingly, with wooden gestures so unlike the sweeping, almost choreographed movements of Chinese desk clerks in Hong Kong, who can pluck a key out of a panel of a thousand boxes almost without looking.

There were approximately 1,500 Chinese staff members at the Great Wall Hotel, who had been chosen from over ten times that number of applicants. With no previous experience in Western hotels or with Western customs, service, or cuisine, and with little foreign-language training, they began to go about their new jobs like artists trying to draw portraits from a verbal description. Although their salaries were substantially higher than they would have been in a government office or factory outside, the real draw of the work was clearly the environment of the hotel itself.

"Most of our staff members are quite young," Hobgood-Brown had told me. "They are clearly dazzled by the idea of working at a place like this, even though many of them are working at rather menial jobs. The men are very proud of their new uniforms, and the women are thrilled to get out of their shapeless Chinese clothes and have their hair cut and permed."

"Could they get any kind of hairdo they wanted?" I inquired.

"Oh no!" said Hobgood-Brown, laughing and shaking her head emphatically. "We had photographs of five officially approved styles which they could choose from. Then we took them over to a hair salon frequented by the diplomatic community and got them all done."

When I asked her how the process of training a staff from the bottom up was going, she smiled and said, "What you have to remember is that before coming here, most of the housekeeping staff had never seen a vacuum cleaner. But considering this lack of experience, I think they have been doing very well, and they are extremely eager to learn."

Wondering how Chinese officials, who not so long ago had been adamant about extirpating every vestige of foreign privilege from China, could now turn around and countenance a luxury hotel for foreigners which effectively excluded Chinese, I asked Hobgood-Brown, as we toured the public rooms one day, if she ever sensed any resentment from the local Chinese staff about the obvious privileges reserved for foreigners here at the Great Wall.

"No, I haven't really," she replied thoughtfully, as our tour took us past the billiard room down toward the hotel's twelve meeting rooms. "For instance, I come to work in a taxi every morning and get reimbursed by the hotel, while all the Chinese staff have to ride to work on bikes or in crowded public buses. You would think that some resentment might develop toward those of us foreigners who have these privileges. But I have not felt any."

When I asked a politically inclined Chinese friend, whose classmate worked at the Great Wall Hotel, if he was aware of any such resentment against the luxuriousness of the life-style offered foreigners, he countered, "How are they going to feel resentment when they are still so happy about getting their jobs? Right now they just want to learn and get ahead. They love working there. It's the next best thing to being in the United States. But what will happen after they've been cleaning rooms and waiting on tables for a few years and actually want to go abroad but can't—I don't know. Maybe then they'll start resenting all the freedom and privileges they see that the foreigners around them have."

Whatever might happen in the future, it was clear that at least at this point in China's reinfatuation with the West, few urban Chinese cared to recall the past, when the inequities between China and the West had played no small role in animating the Chinese Communist movement.

When I later spoke with C. B. Sung, whose Unison International Corporation holds 49 per cent interest in the Great Wall Hotel, I asked if he was concerned lest China's past legacy of anti-foreign feeling might well up once more against such enclaves of privilege. "In the old days, China was more or less a colony of other more powerful countries, and that was a painful experience," he replied. "But today China is independent, and I think it has reached a certain maturity, psychologically speaking. The Chinese have gained a sense of greater international equality, which has helped end the complex of inferiority from which that anti-foreignism often seemed to grow."

How then did he feel Chinese were responding to his new hotel? "I think most Chinese are very proud of it," he answered. "They see it as a real accomplishment for their country to have such a hotel. It is the best in China, and represents a whole new level of attainment for which to strive."

Was he aware of any negative comments? "The only negative remark I have heard was from a pseudo–China expert from the United States," he replied, his voice tinged with a mixture of humor and irritation. "She said that the hotel had no 'Chinese flavor.' But what is 'Chinese flavor' these days? It's cockroaches and ugly, Russian-designed buildings. That's not much to build on."

Almost daily I would spot tour groups of Chinese wearing a look of wonder as they were taken around the hotel. They would troop through the lobby, peer into a lounge or restaurant, or ride on an escalator as if the hotel were one of the revolutionary shrines such as Yan'an, where the Chinese Communists retreated after the Long March; Shaoshan, Mao's birthplace in Hunan; or the old school in Shanghai's

French Concession where the First Party Congress of the Chinese Communist Party was held in 1921, to which such groups once flocked to make obeisances of a different sort.

When I asked Lucy Hobgood-Brown if she thought the hotel would soon become a major tourist destination for curious Chinese, she laughed and replied, "It already has! The Chinese find the hotel extremely interesting and exciting. Of course, they all just love to come in and look around. But there's no way we can accommodate even a small percentage of the people who would like to have a tour. We aren't an industrial exhibit. We just don't have the staff to handle the task, and the hotel can't take it either. They all want to touch everything. There's dust and mud on their shoes. The wear and tear on the rugs alone would be too much." She shook her head, sighed, and then added, "We've asked the Chinese government please to cooperate and limit the number of people they bring through, but still they keep coming. Yesterday, for instance, we had a tour of workers from the factory that made the door knobs for the hotel. We've had a request from the factory that made the nails. Almost all the vice-mayors of Peking have used their influence to get in. Even Party General Secretary Hu Yaobang arrived one day with a huge staff to have a look."

Only a few ordinary residents of Peking will ever get the chance to tour the inside of the hotel, but many can still see it from the outside, and just as a walled garden may evoke a fantasy far more elaborate than anything it actually contains, so the impact of the hotel on those who only see it as they pass by may be even more powerful than on those who actually get inside and in some small measure grow accustomed to it. There are other ways as well that these new hotels exert their influence. For instance, in August, 1984, the State Council announced that fifty Chinese-run hotels throughout China had been "selected" to "try out" the management techniques used by the Peninsula Group at Peking's Jianguo Hotel.

And often I would see Chinese with cameras standing out front in the bitter cold, using the Great Wall Hotel as a backdrop. On one such occasion I met three teachers who were visiting Peking from Sichuan province. They approached and asked me if I would photograph them together. They then moved out onto a divider in the middle of Donghuan North Road, because it afforded the best view of the hotel as a *mise en scène*. When I asked the youngest teacher why they had come all the way to the Great Wall Hotel (a good half-hour by bus from central Peking), he smiled with a suggestion of embarrassment and replied, "Because it's modern." And when I asked him if he knew who owned the hotel, he squinted back at the towering glass high-rise behind him and said, "It looks like it must be an American."

Like earthquakes that send unseen shock waves out through the hardest rock formations hundreds of miles from their epicenters, hotels like the Great Wall are exerting a powerful influence on China. Even though they are walled off from the everyday lives of most Chinese, and even though conservative Party officials are determined to keep them that way, they create dreams by their visible presence, as well as through those Chinese who visit and work there. And just as Chinese have dreamed of the West, whether as a terrifying enemy to be confined or as a potential technological savior, so the West has dreamed of China too. To nineteenth-century Western missionaries, China was millions of potential Christian converts; to its businessmen, untold customers; in more recent times, China has been anything from a billion red ants threatening to destroy the world to a billion staunch socialists, the only hope for its salvation. As few Chinese dreams of the West have been truly satisfied, so Western dreams of China, whether of business or revolution, have fallen terribly short of their hoped-for realization. Yet the dreaming goes on—and once more, as in the nineteenth century, the West, from vantage points like the Great Wall Hotel, is dreaming of China as an endless sinkhole for Western capital and goods; a trading partner par excellence, a billion customers just waiting to drink our Cokes, wear our jeans, buy our factories, power plants, and weapons. From the fantasy island of the hotel, itself a place of dreamy unreality, it is certainly easy to imagine this China. In such a setting—and it is such settings through which Westerners are now increasingly seeing China—it is all too easy to forget that what is actually *out there* is a relatively impoverished country that has historically been either economically self-sufficient or unable to eke out the money to buy an appreciable amount of Western goods; a country that even in 1981 had to back off from its massive modernization program, which overcommitted it to purchases from abroad. History in this sense is not a source of hope; for in the past Western dreams, like Chinese dreams, have more often than not been disappointed.

However, none of this is to say that Westerners and Western-style wares can't capitalize on the current infatuation with things foreign, and be a great moneymaking success in China right now. Taking, for instance, Western food. By 1984, Chinese in Peking had begun to be interested in such strange delicacies as hamburgers and quiche. Whereas previously the capital had only had one "Western-style" restaurant, a dowdy holdover from the days of Sino-Soviet friendship called the Moscow, by the beginning of 1984 it had an increasing number of local restaurants serving Western food, often privately run by enterprising Chinese entrepreneurs taking advantage of the "responsibility system." Although the food in these restaurants seldom bore much resemblance to actual Western food, people flocked to them because there was a certain cachet to dining in such places. One restaurant, the Western Dining Room, which among other things served bread and butter, fried eggs, and "chicken stew," was set up in an underground bomb shelter in the Xidan area adjacent to Democracy Wall (now covered with commercial advertisements rather than wall posters on human rights). Another restaurant served pizza and claimed to offer twenty different kinds of Western cocktails. The New China News Agency, which in the past would have never commented on such enterprises except to condemn them, noted matter-of-factly, "Many Peking residents are now eating Western dinners, and more and more young people have also begun opting for wedding receptions at Western restaurants." The article did not mention it, but young people have also begun opting for Western-style wedding gowns complete with lace veils and long, flowing trains, which can be rented from a growing number of shops throughout the city.

Another Western gastronomical institution gaining popularity in China is American-style white bread. A $1.5 million demonstration white-bread bakery opened in Peking in 1983 as a joint undertaking between the U.S. Wheat Association and the Beijing First Bureau of Light Industry. The new enterprise, which is staffed by four Chinese bakers who attended a twenty-week course at the American Institute of Baking in Manhattan, Kansas, turns out 14,000 loaves of white bread wrapped in American-style plastic bags every day. This has not, however, been enough to keep up with the long lines that form each morning in front of the shops retailing this new-style bread.

"We sell everything we bake, and we can't meet the demand," the deputy manager of the bakery told a Deutsche Presse-Agentur reporter in February, 1984, who went on to note: "The white bread is loved by Chinese who have lived abroad and by the younger generation. They see the new kind of bread as an enrichment of the normal Chinese cuisine, and they get a certain feeling of being 'Western' by eating, for example, white bread and jelly at breakfast." Peking now also has its first "café," the Huagong Western Pastry Shop and Café, which opened a carpeted and air-conditioned shop offering not only Western-style pastry made with butter, but also sandwiches, coffee, and cocoa.

Pizza, cocktails, Western pastries, and white bread with jelly were not the only kinds of Western foods that had begun to invade China as a result of the open door. French *haute cuisine* had also begun to re-establish itself. The Jianguo Hotel had Justine's Restaurant and the Great Wall had La France, both of which served Continental food. But the most interesting new place for gourmet French dining was not inside one of the new hotels but located right in the middle of Chongwenmen, one of Peking's busiest market areas.

The night I went to dine there with two American friends, the piercing winter wind blowing down from Mongolia had almost cleared the streets of pedestrians by seven-thirty. Only an occasional public bus glided past, and a few riders in thick greatcoats and fur-flapped caps drawn down about their ears bent over the handlebars of their bikes were pedalling toward the refuge of their homes. Two horse carts, piled high with straw, moved slowly into the wind like boats struggling up a river against a strong current. Their peasant drivers, wearing layer upon layer of patched, padded clothing, huddled in small concave nests in the straw, looking like religious icons in carved-out niches. All the shops and stores around Chongwenmen were now closed and shielded against the cold by thick quilts that hung down over their doorways. The streets were dark, except for one remaining patch of bright light. On Qianmen Dong Da Jie, just up from the market, floodlights illuminated a red awning that flapped in the wind. On the awning in gold lettering were the words "Maxim's de Paris."

As we approached the entrance, the door sprang open. A young Chinese in a crimson uniform with gold epaulets stood at attention and said in a burry Peking accent, "Bonsoir, messieurs." Stepping from the cold North China night into the warmth and plush decor of Maxim's, where a French hatcheck girl took our coats, was like passing from wakefulness into a dreaming sleep. Upstairs in the salon, a blond, French-speaking waiter wearing a white dinner jacket and carrying a silver tray greeted us and showed us to a table whose centerpiece was a small, gold-leafed candlestick lamp topped by a delicate crenelated shade. The walls were adorned with murals of naked nymphs and sylphs, their vital parts only vaguely rendered so as not to offend Chinese notions of decorum. The ceilings were covered with stained-glass work, giving one the feeling of being inside an oversized Tiffany lamp. The whole room was suffused with soft music from hidden speakers.

The Peking branch of Maxim's is a replica of the famous Parisian restaurant now owned by fashion designer Pierre Cardin. It was installed here in the Chinese capital inside an ordinary-looking high-rise building by French and Japanese decorators in much the same way that surgeons might transplant an organ from one animal into the body of another. "My ambassador doesn't believe it. My friends think I'm mad. But Maxim's is opening in Peking in twenty-four days," Pierre Cardin had announced triumphantly just before his restaurant's debut on October 1, 1983, China's National Day, a time when the whole country celebrates the victory of the Chinese Communist Revolution over the forces of Chiang Kai-shek's army in 1949. "If I can put a Maxim's in Peking, I can put a Maxim's on the moon," he boasted to his guests at the inaugural banquet. "Close your eyes and you are in Paris. It is Paris right down to the smallest detail. . . . China is changing. My idea would have been unthinkable a few years ago. In ten years this country will be like Japan."

Victoria Graham, former Associated Press bureau chief in Peking, who attended the opening, remembers a French diplomat who had lived through the Cultural Revolution in China raising a champagne glass in a toast and enthusiastically proclaiming, "What's happening here is much greater than anything that happened during the Cultural Revolution. It makes me love Deng Xiaoping and his open door."

After drinks in the bar-salon, my friends and I were squired by the blond waiter into the same dining room where that initial banquet had taken place. As we crossed the threshold, a Chinese woman pianist in a formal evening gown and a Chinese male violinist in white tie and tails, both on a small stage, suddenly began to play a Mozart sonata.

Passing a cart laden with French patisseries, fruit tarts, and crème caramel, we were seated with a formal bow at a table set with linen napkins, three sparkling wineglasses at each place, an iced dish of scalloped butter, and a centerpiece of jadelike flowers exquisitely carved out of apples and pears. Having taken our seats, we were handed large menus whose covers were imprinted with a gouache of a Belle Epoque scene from Maxim's in Paris. Consulting the menu, we found such offerings as *coquilles Saint-Jacques provençales*, *crevettes impériales au gratin*, *côtes de veau normande*, and *médaillons de langouste à la mousse de poivrons*, most of which had either been flown in from overseas or shipped in from elsewhere in China in one of Cardin's imported refrigerated vans.

After we ordered, the musicians struck up a Strauss waltz. As we sat drinking a bottle of Pouilly-Fuissé, I looked around the dining room for the first time and realized it was absolutely empty. Thinking that eight o'clock was perhaps too early for Europeans to dine, I concentrated on the wine, assuming that more guests would arrive in due course; but no other guests appeared the whole evening. We dined in magnificent, if self-conscious, solitude. Our only allies in filling the large room with sound were the two musicians; and when they rested, an eerie silence would descend on the room so that each scrape of a fork against a plate, or clink of an ice cube against a glass, was as distinct as the sound of a twig snapping in a still forest.

The tension in the room was palpable. Behind us stood twelve handsome young Chinese waiters—all of whom had been to Paris for apprenticeships at Cardin's flagship restaurant—wearing white ties, tails, and white linen aprons around their waists. They stood stiffly at attention as we ate, their black-and-white uniforms making them appear like a flock of exotically marked but misplaced shorebirds. At the entrance to the dining room stood one other Chinese man.

He wore a double-breasted pinstriped suit that looked as if it might have been made in Shanghai before "liberation." This was Li Jiou Qing, who later introduced himself in somewhat rusty English and French as the "*directeur*" of Maxim's. He was one of the senior Chinese staff members Cardin had found by scouring Peking for waiters and cooks who had worked in Western hotels before 1949 and consequently had some familiarity with the exacting demands of first-class French cuisine and service.

The formality, the imported wine, the French food, the classical music, and the turn-of-the-century Parisian decor all conspired to create an environment so disconnected from the People's Republic of China that I felt as if we were on a stage enacting a strange and absurd drama for which there was no script, and no audience but the restaurant staff.

When Pierre Cardin was planning his Peking branch of Maxim's, he was asked by a Reuters reporter whether or not he had done any market studies before beginning to transplant this replica of his rue Royale restaurant to Peking. "Statistics don't interest me," retorted Cardin cavalierly. "I've made front-page news for forty years now, which proves that I've succeeded. For the moment, I don't know whether I will make profits. But if I make profits, the Chinese will profit too."

If my evening at Maxim's was any indication, it would appear that Cardin's immediate chances of earning a profit from his restaurant were negligible; but Cardin, who had told the same reporter that "Maxim's was a place where you can dream," appeared to have other dreams of his own. Maxim's was for now simply a means for Cardin to stake out territory in China and leave his mark. Cardin's·real dreams were of expanding, ultimately to sell food and clothing to "the man in the street," as he put it. "I am aiming at the biggest market in the world—China," he said, grandiloquently evoking the dreams of nineteenth-century English merchants who had hoped to keep the mills of Lancashire turning forever by persuading every "Chinaman" to add one inch to his shirt tail. But the dreams that came to me in Cardin's restaurant were not of trade or even Paris. Between a course of *fois gras frais maison* and a *filet de boeuf Stroganoff*, I walked alone to the washroom, trying to imagine the Chinese who lived just beyond Maxim's walls in their small, freezing rooms with no conception of the luxurious world that lay within this building. Then I thought of Mao Zedong lying in repose inside his massive mausoleum only a short distance away. What would that sage of Chinese Communism have made of Maxim's de Beijing?

Had he decided to make an inspection tour, would he simply have handed his familiar cap and coat to the French hatcheck girl as other Chinese officials had done more recently when invited by foreigners to dine at Maxim's? And how would he have responded when he ascended the staircase to the bar and heard the strains of Mozart and Strauss being played by two of his minions dressed up like a nineteenth-century French *comte* and *comtesse*, and then seen twelve young Chinese in European formal dinner wear pouring imported wine into crystal glasses for wealthy foreigners? Might he not have retreated behind the vermilion walls of his quarters at Zhongnanhai and launched another cultural revolution? Might not his followers, now hidden in the woodwork, someday have the power to do the same, once again disappointing the hopes and dreams of the West and those Chinese who are drawn by its powerful magnetism? Might not the dreams embodied in Maxim's and other possibly more practical Western projects prove, in the long term, a terribly fragile structure on the tumultous Chinese body politic?

However, as we finished our $160 dinner with a *mousse glacée aux framboises* and paid with an American Express card—the first time I had ever been able to use a credit card in China—Chairman Mao's era as Great Helmsman seemed as remote from the present as that of the mythological Yellow Emperor, who is said to have lived back in the mists of Chinese prehistory. As we returned to the bar for after-dinner drinks, I noticed out of the corner of my eye that one by one the waiters were emerging from a room behind the bar, now stripped of their formal attire and once again garbed in bulky Chinese street clothes for the chilly trip home. One young man, his head so wrapped in scarves that he looked like a bandaged battle casualty, carried a large thermos bottle in which he was undoubtedly taking home some hot water, a luxury few Chinese have in their flats yet unless they heat it on their stoves. In the bar we met Monsieur Humbert des Lyons de Feuchin, the manager of Maxim's de Paris à Pékin. Sitting down at our table, this well-groomed Frenchman, who looked to be in his late thirties, summoned a bottle of imported champagne. As we drank, I asked him if he did not sometimes feel in an anomalous position here in China.

"Yes, it is extraordinary to be here," began de Feuchin, losing some of his reserve. "A short while ago there was no place to go to eat well in Peking. And now look!" he said, gesturing expansively around him. "It's absolutely fantastic with Maxim's and the Great Wall and Jianguo hotels here!"

As we chatted, de Feuchin told me that Maxim's in Peking was only one of a string of Cardin restaurants around the world, including branches in Brussels, Mexico City, Tokyo, London, and Rio, with one under negotiation in Moscow, and another due to open in New York at the end of 1984. The Peking Maxim's, he told me, was a joint venture between Groupe Cardin Maxim's, which paid for all the equipment and did the interior decoration, and the Second Bureau of the Beijing Municipality, which supplied the building. (It also houses the China International Travel Service.)

I asked de Feuchin if he had had any trouble working out the running of the restaurant with his Chinese counterparts.

"Well, of course we must discuss everything with them before we do it," he replied. "For instance, we had to ask the Second Bureau for permission to have dancing here on Saturday nights. They thought about it for a while and then finally gave their permission. So for the first time, this past

New Year's night, we had dancing until 5:15 A.M.," continued de Feuchin, with a look of proprietary satisfaction.

Did he have any apprehensions that Maxim's might ever become the target of some future campaign against foreigners or "spiritual pollution"?

"No. Most Chinese don't know what's inside here, and anyway, I think they understand it is not a place for them to come into unless accompanied by a foreigner."

De Feuchin's statement soon became only partially true, for in the summer of 1984 Cardin opened a second restaurant, downstairs from Maxim's, which he called Minim's. Minim's is a fast-food outlet with much more affordable prices (no hard currency needed), designed to introduce the Chinese masses to crèpes, quiche, croissants, patisserie, and coffee. Minim's was not, however, the capital's first restaurant serving Western-style fast food. For in April, 1984, the Yi Li ("Righteous Advantage") Restaurant opened under the tutelage of several fast-food counselors from Hong Kong in the heart of Peking, the first of three planned take-out establishments marked by an unusual logo: a Donald Duck figurine standing on its roof. The Yi Li serves hamburgers, hot dogs, french fries, pepper steak, ice cream, and french toast, along with assorted Chinese dishes.

I asked de Feuchin why he thought the Chinese had allowed Cardin to create two such restaurants in their midst.

Giving a shrug, he replied, "They appreciate Pierre Cardin. They like the business he brings them."

When a similarly perplexed Western reporter asked Chen Muhua, China's Minister for Economic Relations and Trade, how her government could ideologically justify the presence of Maxim's in a socialist country, she replied, "Eating is something that belongs to culture, not communism or capitalism. So, why not Maxim's?" Evidently Party General Secretary Hu Yaobang agreed. For on June 14, 1984, he invited writer Harrison Salisbury—who was researching a book on the Long March—and China hand John Service to dinner at his residential compound in Peking's Zhongnanhai, where he served them truffle soup, lobster salad, escargots, steak, and ice cream. To my knowledge this was the first Western meal served by China's Communist leadership in decades.

Cardin himself first burst on the Chinese scene in December, 1978, when he spent a week visiting nine textile factories in Tianjin, Hangzhou, Peking, and Shanghai. Before returning to Paris he had been appointed by the Chinese government as consultant to the Chinese National Import-Export Company for Textile Products (Chinatex). He was also asked to return to China the following March to show his own ready-to-wear collection in Peking and Shanghai.

"It's not a matter of China awakening, it's more a case of China exploding," said Cardin exuberantly, back in Paris. "There are a billion people out there who need clothes. I am the first one to go into China."

Did Pierre Cardin, who already had a mini-empire that employed over 15,000 people and sold its products in over one hundred countries, really expect to make money in China with a restaurant that was often empty and a line of clothing fashions that many Chinese officials view as subversive and decadent?

"He takes the long view," I was told by Madame Sung Huai-kuei, a Chinese-born artist who emigrated to Europe with her Bulgarian husband in 1974, and who has now returned to Peking as business representative for Cardin's China interests. "He realizes that the Party wants to make money for China. He is not averse to making money himself. But he is an artist as well as a businessman, and this is something these Chinese officials do not always grasp. Cardin sees China as a vast sleeping place that he would like to artistically awaken. He is like a sculptor who, when he sees a magnificent piece of uncut stone, cannot resist wanting to carve it."

"But isn't Cardin's conception of the finished Chinese

sculpture somewhat different from that of China's Party leaders?" I asked.

"Ah, well," Madame Sung responded, shrugging and giving a sweet laugh. "But never mind. Cardin likes to do difficult things. He looks at China and sees so many beautiful people in such terrible clothes. That provokes him. He wants to do something about it. The fact that it looks impossible only makes him want to do it more. For him, China is the perfect challenge."

Some Chinese, however, were not certain that they wanted to become the perfect challenge for a French clothes designer. The first stirrings of fashion consciousness in China provoked a reaction against exactly the kinds of things Cardin wanted to bring into their country. In March, 1979, several days before Cardin arrived back in China for his first shows, the *Peking Daily* published two letters from older workers criticizing the way many young people had already begun to fixate on Western fashions. "Seeing the behavior of certain young people, we older workers are worried," said one letter. "These young people have not thoroughly studied literature, Marxism-Leninism and Mao Zedong Thought. Instead of devoting themselves to work, these young people prefer to wear pornographic bell-bottom trousers, spend hours getting their hair permed, and excite themselves doing foreign dances. Such behavior really should not be permissible."

Cardin may have been entering the "biggest market in the world," but not everyone in it was ready to embrace the importation of foreign fashion. Even the most elite Chinese had been stylistically dormant for three decades. Nonetheless, Cardin arrived with twenty French and Japanese models in March, 1979, to present his most current line of clothing to a Chinese audience. Many of Cardin's new creations presented what some Western critics then called his "superman" look, namely, oversized shoulders. Among other designs he showed a shimmery black bodysuit topped with a pink cape. An article on this pathbreaking show in the *Hong Kong Standard* was headlined CARDIN GREETED WITH ASTOUNDED SILENCE.

Christopher Pritchett, a Peking-based Reuters correspondent, filed the following account: "Slinky French models slid along Peking's first catwalk tonight, and hundreds of Chinese gasped in disbelief and sometimes in horror. After turning a drab meeting hall into a hideaway with bright lights and loud pop music, designer Pierre Cardin let loose with a flight of fantasy to show the Chinese textile industry what he could do with his products.

"He also managed to convey the impression that people would have the shape of inverted pyramids; extremely broad shoulders turned up to a peak for both men and women, and narrow waists were Cardin's favorite theme. So were naked shoulders, leg displays and glimpses of forbidden territory that the 400-member audience looked at open-mouthed. Nothing like it has ever been seen in drab Peking. Some of the women covered their faces and tittered. The men looked at the ceiling when they could tear their eyes away from all the flesh."

"It was quite a shock when the Chinese first saw our clothes in 1979," Madame Sung told me as she reminisced over a cup of tea in the Peking Hotel. "I think they felt that the designs were very strange and not at all beautiful. But, you know, since then things have changed rapidly. Now young Chinese women will see me on the street in my Cardin dresses, and they will stop me and say, 'Oh, how beautiful! Where can we buy such clothes?'

"For thirty years styles did not change in China," she continued reflectively, her long, elegantly coiffed hair and understated but lovely Cardin dress giving her an emphatically Western air. "I think the uniformity and repetition made everyone quite psychologically depressed. Now China wants to modernize. But as long as there are such limits on the imagination, I don't see how the Chinese people can ever really be free to create a new and vibrant country."

Pierre Cardin was not the only Western fashion designer to be invited to China right after the annunciation of Deng Xiaoping's new "open-door" policy. In September of 1980, Halston, accompanied by Bianca Jagger and his "Halston-ettes" (twelve top-paid New York models), made a $600,000 tour of three continents and numerous countries, including China. Halston, like Cardin, had been invited by Chinatex to Peking and Shanghai in the hope of further developing overseas markets for Chinese textiles and finished garments.

In Peking, Halston visited the Great Wall and proclaimed, "I think it is a great wall," in response to questions by foreign correspondents. Bianca Jagger was reported to have carved some graffiti on the stonework of the ancient edifice and then to have visited the Forbidden City, strolling among the old Imperial palaces in bare feet, a braless top, and a pair of skintight black leather pants. Prior to departing for Shanghai, where the fashion show was scheduled to take place, Halston announced to the Halstonettes that he wanted everyone to arrive attired in Mao jackets and hats and, in the words of *Women's Wear Daily*, "accessorized with Halston red cosmetics and Peretti compacts."

The fashion show itself took place before 1,400 employees from the Chinese textile and garment workers' unions in the Shanghai Exhibition Hall. Their reactions varied from polite admiration to outright dismay as the Halstonettes twirled about in an assortment of plunging necklines and other revealing styles. The *pièces de résistance* of the show were a see-through jumpsuit and blouse, both made of dark net, which left the audience aghast and caused one Chinese viewer to suggest that the wearers belonged in a mental hospital rather than in a fashion show.

When informed that a Halston gown could cost as much as $10,000, another Chinese in the audience was reported to have exclaimed incredulously, "That could feed an entire village so easily!" When an embarrassed young Chinese woman in the audience was persuaded to try on a lavish full-length Halston evening gown with a red-ruffled skirt over her Chinese sweater and trousers, Halston pronounced that he "found Chinese women to be very beautiful. And the Chinese people—as I have observed them—are pure, innocent, and good."

During the show, Bianca Jagger was seen leaning nonchalantly against a pillar wearing a high-collared Chinese Mao jacket and a blue cap with a red star. After the official Chinese banquet that followed the fashion show, she was reported by *Women's Wear Daily* to have headed out on her own for a tour of Shanghai in full evening regalia. Wearing a flowing white evening dress and gold tiara, she spent two hours walking the streets of the city. It is unlikely that those Chinese who encountered her while peddling home on their bikes from a late factory shift will readily forget the image.

Pierre Cardin returned to Peking for a second show in 1981, and then for a third one in 1983, just before the gala opening banquet at Maxim's. This time, instead of bringing foreign models to show his collection, he arranged to use twenty-five young Chinese from the Beijing East City Cultural Palace's Clothing Exhibition School. The showing of Western fashions by Chinese models was in its own way as big a milestone in China's accommodation to Western design as Cardin's invitation in the first place. For in allowing Chinese to be seen in public in avant-garde Western clothing, China's leaders were in effect giving their tacit approval for another quantum leap forward in the absorption of Western style by the Chinese garment industry.

As Madame Sung told me in one of our evening talks, "It was symbolically an important thing for Cardin to be allowed to use Chinese girls as models. They themselves were at first very nervous about wearing Western clothes in public even for an official occasion. But you know, they have now already grown accustomed to them. In fact, they love Cardin's designs so much now that I don't think they could ever go back to Chinese clothes." To express his gratitude,

Cardin gave each of the young models a gift of new European-made shoes and a set of underwear—which were, however, immediately confiscated by Chinese authorities.

The confiscation of Cardin's presents seemed to express perfectly the ambivalence the Chinese leadership was collectively feeling about what they had started to unleash: namely, a miniature liberation of Chinese aesthetic sensibilities (albeit with a strong measure of stylistic borrowing from abroad). On the one hand, they had evidently decided that Chinese garment workers needed to learn from the West in order to modernize the Chinese textile industry and compete on the world market. This meant that a certain amount of familiarity with Western fashion techniques was unavoidable. Hence, people like Cardin and Halston were invited to China, much in the way that experts in hydroelectric projects or oil exploration might be brought in to advise on technical matters. But there seemed to be little initial appreciation of the subversive role that fashion could play in such a society, being, as it was, one of the consummate expressions of aesthetic individualism in the West. China's leaders seemed to have the quaint idea that aspects of Western fashion could be detached from the Western value system out of which they had grown; that they could be borrowed like a computer and plugged in to serve the Chinese Revolution without any broader cultural impact.

Chinese officialdom might embrace Cardin as a technician who could teach them something about designing marketable clothing, but many were hardly enthusiastic about Cardin the "artist" or "sculptor," as Madame Sung had described him, who, figuratively speaking, wished to carve the "magnificent piece of uncut stone" that was China. In fashion, as in other sorts of technological borrowing from abroad, Party leaders seemed to believe that they could maintain the fiction of being in control of the flow of the contaminating values that were inclined to accompany modern technology and technocrats by concocting formulas

148

that divided Western influences up into good and bad, and proclaiming that they would allow only those influences that were not "bourgeois" or "decadent" to enter the country. Party leaders seemed to imagine that where there once had been a barrier, they could now simply interpose a filter across the new "open door" which would allow them to take "the best from East and West": to absorb the technology China needed to modernize, while extracting the bourgeois impurities and disposing of them before they corrupted the Chinese people. "Use foreign things to serve China," proclaimed the Party, reviving an old Maoist slogan.

This was, of course, not the first time the Chinese had endeavored to borrow know-how from the West while rejecting the value system out of which it had grown. In the nineteenth century, after repeated defeats at the hands of Western powers, progressive scholar-officials of the Qing dynasty—who came to be known as "self-strengtheners"— endeavored to formulate theories of their own which justified the importation of Western science and technology while protecting Confucian civilization from the ravages of subversive "barbarian" values. Zhang Zhidong, one of the foremost "self-strengtheners," tried to distinguish "practical" things like science and technology from "essential" or "spiritual" things like values and culture. "*Zhongxue weiti, Xixue weiyong*," he proclaimed. "Use Chinese learning for matters of spiritual essence, and use Western learning for matters pertaining to practical use." The "self-strengtheners" hoped to protect China's traditional cultural identity from erosion while borrowing Western technology to build arsenals, railroads, steamships, and telegraph systems, just as China's leaders now hoped to borrow such things as computer technology, industrial management, hotel science, and even fashion to modernize their country without fatally impairing the values of their "socialist spiritual civilization." But as the translator and philosopher Yan Fu, one of China's early advocates of Westernization, had said in criticizing Zhang's *ti* and *yong* formulation at the turn of the century when China was involved in an earlier frenzy of Western borrowing, "I have never heard that the left hand and right hand can be considered respectively as fundamental principles and application."

Whatever new skills the Western fashion industry may offer a China desperate to create exports that will earn foreign currency, Western fashion itself, even more than the other byproducts of foreign technology and capital, is an infectious phenomenon. It is such a visible cultural form that almost anyone can appreciate it. Particularly in a country like China, which has been aesthetically starved for so long, and where there has been so little variety of color and design in personal dress, the presentations of Western fashions were bound to burst like bombs, suddenly throwing the whole world of plain Chinese clothing into stark relief and breaking the bounds of Party containment. Indeed, once young Chinese got a taste of fashion and of lavishing attention on themselves rather than the masses, their enthusiasm was not easy to contain.

The visits of Western fashion designers like Cardin and Halston were only one impetus among many that caused this revival not only in Chinese fashion and design but in the way the Chinese were beginning once again self-consciously to view themselves—and the Party found itself forced to shift, however laboriously, with the times. "We must design more beautiful, tasteful, and popular dresses so that our women will be more beautifully attired," Shanghai dress designer Gu Xirong told one Chinese reporter by way of extolling the 160 new women's garment designs that went on sale in Shanghai stores during the summer of 1979. Just a month after Cardin's first pathbreaking fashion show in Peking, a team of seventeen hair stylists from Austria, Australia, Mexico, England, Japan, and Hong Kong and two senior beauticians from Max Factor arrived in China on a consulting tour arranged by the Pivot International Hair Designers Club and the International Beauty Group in

Hong Kong. The tour stopped in Canton, Shanghai, and Peking to do hair-styling and makeup demonstrations.

By the fall, fashion billboards had begun to spring up in China, even on Changan Boulevard, which runs past not only the Imperial City but Zhongnanhai, the Great Hall of the People, and Tiananmen Square, where Mao lies in his mausoleum on public view. These new advertisements stood in garish contrast to the massive, hairy portraits of Marx, Lenin, Engels, and Stalin that had kept watch over the Gate of Heavenly Peace, along with the red-and-white billboards that for the last several decades had proclaimed such messages as LONG LIVE THE CHINESE COMMUNIST PARTY; WORKERS OF THE WORLD, UNITE; and other sayings culled from the works of Chairman Mao. One of seven new billboards put up by Chinatex showed a young Chinese woman with pink lips, nail polish, and permed hair rubbing her cheek against a Snow Lotus–brand sweater. The caption read: "Smooth, silky feeling, velvety softness, elaborate workmanship, smart-looking, warm, comfortable, and durable. Orders welcome in both English and Chinese."

In 1979, the Shanghai Fashion Design Institute, China's first modelling troupe, was set up and began recruiting fashion models from among textile-mill workers in the area. Collectively referred to as the "fashion demonstration team," the institute soon had 260 employees. As the *China Daily* explained, models "must have attractive facial features and the body type required to show off clothing: wide shoulders and narrow waists for men, well-rounded figures and delicate hands for women." In 1980, China got its first of several clothing design magazines, a quarterly called *Fashion*, which featured color photographs of Chinese, Japanese, and Western models wearing long dresses, tailored suits, slacks, and jewelry. Put out by the Foreign Trade Publishing House, *Fashion* was an immediate hit.

Each time I returned to China in the late nineteen-seventies and early nineteen-eighties, the changes that had taken place in people's dress styles while I had been absent were immediately apparent. The effect was something like looking at one of Eadweard Muybridge's series of time-sequence photographs of running animals with intermittent frames removed. Suddenly in 1979, for instance, some young men began to acquire a faintly hoody look as they rushed to buy foreign sunglasses after the American series "Man from Atlantis" appeared on Chinese television. Some youths even began to wear long, shaggy hair and to appear in bell-bottom pants, Western suit jackets, and an occasional trenchcoat or cape.

By the nineteen-eighties I began to notice women wearing more splashes of color, perhaps a brightly colored blouse or scarf. The more audacious began to appear in public during the summer in short-sleeved cotton dresses. Stylish bonnets soon appeared in great numbers. Hair salons, which had previously been confined to large hotels patronized by Western tourists, suddenly began opening all across China, and were soon flooded with young women poring over photographs of Western and Hong Kong models before getting their own hair permed. China's burgeoning tonsorial industry had a culmination of sorts in May, 1983, when a hairdressing exhibition was held in a downtown Peking park. Almost a hundred new hairstyles went on display. The most popular style was called "the Seagull" because of the way the hair, curling out from the sides of the head, suggested a gull about to take off.

By 1983, the Chinese had also started to hold fashion and clothing shows of their own, albeit less daring than those of Cardin and Halston. In March, the Ministry of Textile Industry sponsored a twenty-nine-day sales exhibition of spring and summer clothing at the Peking Exhibition Center. The *China Daily* described it as "wildly popular" and as a "renaissance of stylish, colorful clothes and a budding fashion industry."

"This is the dawn of the golden age of fashion in China,"

proclaimed Quan Shiping, the shipping director of the People's Garment Factory, one of the Chinese clothing enterprises showing its new styles at the exhibit. Each day more than 13,000 Chinese elbowed their way around the exhibit, so that by the time the show had ended almost half a million people had had a chance to view the more than four thousand varieties of clothing inside. Tickets for the show were so much in demand that scalpers were able to sell them for fifty times their original price. Moreover, the exhibit was visited by none other than Premier Zhao Ziyang, Vice-Premier Yao Yilin, and Chairman Peng Zhen of the Standing Committee of the National People's Congress, as well as many other high-ranking officials. Ordinary customers who were fortunate enough to get into the exhibit bought 1.2 million garments worth 10 million yuan, including sleeveless dresses, safari jackets, brightly colored body stockings, jogging suits, and synthetic Georgette crepe blouses.

Factories that had not restyled their clothing from the baggy unisex look of years past made few sales at the exhibit, and soon found their warehouses piling up with unsold merchandise. When asked to explain this dramatic shift in buyer preference, Quan Shiping told a *China Daily* reporter: "What happened was that customers became more selective. For years people just bought whatever they could find in order to have something to wear. But by two years ago everyone had enough clothes, and since there was nothing new on the market, they stopped buying."

Quan, who had been on a six-month visit to Japan, was distressed by the image of Chinese clothes abroad. "Even in crowded areas like the Ginza [Tokyo's main shopping district] you could pick out Chinese people at a glance," he said disparagingly. "They seemed to walk sluggishly, and they all wore baggy pants and jackets with short sleeves and long bodies. What's more, the clothes were all the same color, usually gray or blue." Then, as if he might have gone too far without making the proper genuflection to socialist ideology, Quan added dutifully, "Of course, beautification of the mind must be given priority. But looking nice is also important."

In May, Peking hosted its first all-Chinese fashion show, put on by the Fashion Design Institute in Shanghai. A troupe of twenty-four models from the Institute showed residents of the capital nearly one hundred new Shanghai designs for women's garments. The *Economic Daily* proclaimed that the show had helped put a "wholesome and solemn" new fashion industry back on its feet in China.

"Wholesome and solemn" were interesting words to use in describing China's new fashion industry in Shanghai, a city rapidly regaining its former reputation as the fashion capital of China. Whether Shanghai would ever actually reach the same level of fashion consciousness that it had had before "liberation" in 1949 was doubtful. At that time, although Shanghai was well known for the poverty-stricken condition of its lower classes, a whole wealthy segment of Chinese society dressed almost exclusively in stylish Western clothes, dined at Western restaurants, and frequented the city's many chic European-run nightclubs. So Westernized in dress and manner did many of these Chinese become that China's great essayist and short-story writer Lu Xun contemptuously referred to them as "phony foreign devils," suggesting that by so completely aping Western styles, they had forsaken their Chinese roots and lost their native identities.

By 1984, it seemed as if almost every other day some new fashion event was taking place in Peking, which has long been known as one of China's most conservative large cities. After each event, those involved in the Chinese world of design seemed to grow bolder and more confident that what they were doing now actually had a future and would not necessarily bommerang back on them in some new campaign against "bourgeois decadence" or "capitalist roaders."

In July, 1983, China held a fashion contest. Sponsored by *Fashion* magazine, the First National Fashion Design

Competition solicited entries from all over the country. Six winners were chosen from the 2,200 entries by a panel of judges including two Japanese designers. The winner was Yao Hong, a twenty-year-old woman from the Beijing Children's Clothing Workshop. Her winning entry was a floor-length white satin gown with a cascade of colorful ribbing down one side and a puff of embroidered clouds on the skirt. Yao was awarded a certificate of merit, a cash prize, and a scholarship to study in Japan for six months.

In July of 1984, the Beijing Workers Committee and the *Beijing Daily* joined to sponsor an exhibit called "New China, New Beijing," which included a fashion show featuring models in tight-fitting *qipaos*—made famous in the West by the movie *The World of Suzie Wong* and long forbidden in China—slit up the thighs, high heels, pearl necklaces, earrings, and designer handbags. A few days later, another fashion show was held in Beijing featuring more chic Chinese models wearing jazzy Mao suits, miniskirts, evening gowns, heavy makeup, and mirrored sunglasses—all parading before the crowd to the sounds of Michael Jackson and his band.

Fashion, which had begun its comeback as a technical skill for professionals in the Chinese textile and clothing industry, was clearly by the end of 1984 spilling out into the population at large, in a way that surprised and gratified some Chinese while shocking and dismaying others. Like almost every other aspect of China's modernization program, this resurgence of fashion was raising contradictions that were hard to overlook. The most obvious among them was that this liberation of Chinese aesthetics was in stark opposition to Mao Zedong's notion that art of any kind was justifiable only if it advanced the cause of socialist revolution. As he told his people in his seminal lectures on art and literature in Yan'an in 1942: "There is in reality no such thing as art for art's sake, art that stands above classes, or art that runs parallel to or remains independent of politics. . . . Art and literature are subordinate to politics, but they in turn also exert a great influence on politics. Revolutionary art and literature are part of the entire cause of the revolution; they are its cogs and screws . . . indispensable to the whole machine, and form an indispensable part of the entire cause of the revolution."

Now, however, even radio and television were beginning to include fashion programming with no evident redeeming political importance. In October, 1983, Hunan Provincial Television ran a month-long series entitled "On the Beauty of Clothing," which featured young workers, actresses, clothing designers, and teachers discussing their personal views on fashion. Hunan is, of course, Mao Zedong's natal province, and it has recently been a stronghold of Maoist leftism. Nonetheless, participants defended jeans, bell-bottom trousers, and other so-called exotic clothes, claiming that such new styles, far from being counter-revolutionary, actually expressed young people's daring to probe the unknown—almost a parody of Mao's famous dictum of the Cultural Revolution, "Dare to rebel." One interviewee noted philosophically that often fashions viewed as extreme at one point in time end up becoming common, everyday apparel later on. Tang Yubing, a clothing designer with the Changsha Garment Corporation, tried to reconcile both extremes by saying, "There is no reason why people cannot wear jeans and colored shirts," hastily adding, however, that "clothing that exposes the bosom, back, and shoulders is not suited to Chinese customs and will not be popular."

In a commentary on this unusual show, the New China News Agency noted pragmatically that "besides helping to dispel misgivings about stylish clothing, the television discussions have also resulted in a minor bonanza for garment shops." This bonanza was not limited to the sale of casual clothing alone. Work clothes for the Chinese laboring masses also began to be influenced by new design concepts. In January, 1984, the Ministry of Commerce sponsored a show in Peking of newly designed work clothes including a stylish sky-blue apron for barbers, uniforms in beige tints for textile workers, a selection of brightly colored overalls for factory workers, and clothing made from dirt-resistant fabric for street cleaners and sanitation workers.

All over China different forces of government workers began to shed their "baggies" (as one American friend of mine called them) and to appear in smart new regimental dress, which often had obvious similarities to uniforms worn by government workers abroad. For instance, China's customs officials showed up for work one day in stylish black uniforms and caps almost identical to those worn by their Hong Kong counterparts across the border. Traffic police were recycled into military-style uniforms that looked as if they might have been inspired by the Soviet Army. After the Jianguo Hotel in Peking had been open awhile, the staff at the Chinese-run Peking Hotel appeared in new uniforms that were clearly derivative; while airline hostesses, who once patrolled the aisles of planes in shapeless gray tunics, appeared now in tailored trousers and jackets topped off at mealtimes with frilly pink aprons.

A fashion-conscious metalworker even wrote in to the *China Daily*, complaining that while other workers had been given "trim uniforms with shiny buttons and bright shoulder loops," his colleagues were still wearing clothing "designed decades ago" that was "loose-fitting and cumbersome." He went on to lament that "everyone wearing them, whether male or female, resembles a slovenly dressed grandpa or grandma." He concluded his plea for sartorial equality by proclaiming, in a tone that sounded almost like a Red Guard resolutely demanding an end to China's feudal class system, "I believe that metallurgical workers have every reason to demand a reform of their ugly work clothes."

Clothing for children also began to be affected by this new fascination with fashion. In June, 1984, Shanghai Television celebrated the thirty-fifth anniversary of the founding of the Chinese Young Pioneers with a children's clothing competition. On a program called "Friendly Advice," children between the ages of four and eight appeared on camera modelling clothing designed by their parents. These young mannequins included the children of several foreigners living in Shanghai.

Some Chinese even began to express concern that China's older people were being left behind by the rising tide of fashion. One such person wrote to the *China Daily* in the spring of 1984, complaining that it was "easier to buy fashionable clothes for young people than for the old, even though many of them want to wear attractive clothing. Unfortunately, the only choice available for them is the dull-colored tunic uniform."

For the first time, television newscasters began to appear on the screen in Western suits and ties. Slowly, more and more ordinary Chinese men began to buy such attire and to wear it in public. The *Yangcheng Evening News* in Canton even carried an article impugning the "Mao suit" as "impractical," and suggesting that Western clothes conferred a "dynamic appearance" on those Chinese who wore them, echoing in a small way the sentiments of the nineteenth-century Westernizer Yan Fu, who at the turn of the century first spoke in admiration of the dynamic, Promethean energy of the West.

Western clothing received its biggest official boost when Premier Zhao Ziyang arrived in the United States for a state visit in January, 1984, wearing a suit and tie himself, something that would have seemed inconceivable when Deng visited the United States in 1979. Whether Premier Zhao imagined that his own suit and tie would bestow on him a "dynamic appearance" is not known, but in an article that appeared in the *China Daily*, a Chinese reporter travelling with him wrote that the Premier had made a "good impression" on Americans. He claimed that "Americans from taxi drivers to good personal friends remarked that his wearing a tie and a Western suit projected an image that he was someone with whom Americans can easily 'get along and talk with,' because 'he didn't look so different.' "

When Zhao was asked at a New York banquet by CBS news anchor Diane Sawyer whether any political significance could be imputed to his choice of clothing styles, he launched into a discourse on fashion, saying, "I am also in favor of ladies beautifying themselves. They can wear lipstick and earrings, and rearrange hairstyles. This is not part of cultural pollution. In the past in China, you felt it was difficult to distinguish women from men, since they all wore the same-color "Mao suit.' Now you'll see that the dresses in Peking are more colorful. This will make you very glad, and I am also glad to see it."

Zhao could hardly have thought of a more graphic way to disassociate himself from the Maoist phase of China's Revolution. He was, of course, observed on television in his new apparel by hundreds of millions of Chinese back home. What was he telling them? That to be modern was now acceptable even if it meant capitulating in some measure to Western styles? But how far could average Chinese expect to "modernize" their own lives without running afoul of Party prohibitions against "bourgeois liberalism"? It was a question of degree that, as always, was difficult to discern. Nonetheless, the image of the Premier of China wearing a Western suit and tie in the United States of America was a powerful one.

It just so happened that while Zhao was abroad, a show began back home in Shanghai featuring 170 new styles of Western suits manufactured in local factories. The day it opened, 10,000 Chinese attended the show and bought 34,000 yuan worth of apparel, and a short but telling item in the *Yangcheng Evening News* reported that during the first twelve days of February (immediately following Zhao's return from the United States), Canton's Nanfang Mansion Department Store had sold 13,000 neckties to Chinese youths, many of whom came from rural areas. What was going on? Why should the Party have allowed the old "Mao suit," which had become so closely identified with the Chinese Revolution, to slip off so quickly into historical oblivion? Why was the Chinese Communist Party, which had spent thirty years promoting conformity and unity among its people, now allowing, even promoting, a force as potentially disruptive as fashion?

For one thing, in addition to modernizing China's textile industry, this flirtation with modern Western fashion was a fast way to image-make: to let it be known at home that a new era had begun, and to reassure foreign businessmen that the Chinese were becoming more like them and thus once again trustworthy in the international marketplace. There may also have been a segment of the leadership which shared Madame Sung's rather Western conviction that the real energy and imagination of the Chinese people would never be fully released until some measure of artistic freedom and self-expression was allowed. But it would be deceptive, I think, to see China's reimmersion in fashion as a real invitation from the leadership to the Chinese people to indulge in unrestrained self-expression. For the truth was that even with all their reformist zeal, Deng and most other Party leaders still remained utterly unwilling to release the Party's ultimate controlling hand. As long as the development of fashion in China remained epiphenomenal, and as long as a limited permission for the Chinese people to dress up could bestow the luster of modernity on the Deng regime, it could be tolerated, but where the Party was involved, there were limits to flexibility. Young people might be relieved to find themselves granted a new measure of freedom in fashion, but they would have been wrong to interpret it as a wholesale invitation to do away with all of China's revolutionary iconography. Like everything else in China, fashion too was a political football that played into factional disputes. Deng was more than willing to use fashion in his ongoing struggle against old-line Maoists, but if fashion began to become a liability in this political battle, he was far from averse to turning against it. Had Deng not come to power in the late seventies supported by the youths of the Democracy Wall Movement, who decried the dictatorial manner of the Party under the Gang of Four and then-Party Chairman Hua Guofeng? And hadn't Deng at first encouraged these young idealists and even proclaimed their right to put up critical wall posters when he himself was struggling against entrenched Party power, saying, "We should not check the demands of the masses to speak?" However, once his own position was secure as paramount leader of China, what had he done? He had revoked the "Four Greats," which guaranteed the freedom to speak, discuss, put up wall posters, and hold debates, and then turned on his former young allies. In a matter of months Deng had arrested most of them and either put them on trial and imprisoned them or shipped them off to labor reform camps.

Like freedom of speech in 1978 and 1979, fashion in the early eighties was enjoying a springtime of sorts. Since periods of liberalization have a way of expanding and then suddenly contracting in China, no one could be sure how long it would last, but as it continued into the fall of 1983, I was constantly surprised by the amount of support the development of fashion received from both unofficial and official sources. Even the *People's Daily* seemed to be warmed by the existence of this mini-movement. In July of 1983, one commentator reflected on the situation with surprising sympathy: "Monotonous colors and outdated styles remained unchanged for years. People ridiculed us, saying that blue, gray, and black were our national colors. . . . [But now] along the crowded downtown streets, among the customary blues, whites, and grays one can see yellows, reds, pinks, greens, and purples. It gives one the happy feeling that in recent years the people's living standard has really improved."

One other very obvious manifestation of how the "people's living standard" had improved was the revival of the cosmetics industry in China. While Mao and his wife Jiang Qing still ruled, just about the only cosmetic one could find in stores was cold cream. By 1984, this situation had changed dramatically. For instance, China's domestic perfume industry, which had languished since 1966 when Mao called Red Guards out to "bombard the headquarters" of the Communist Party bureaucracy, suddenly began to produce again. In May, 1982, a commentary in the *People's Daily* even took up its defense. Without passing judgment on whether or not it was politically correct for Chinese women to use perfume, it noted practically that "many goods such as perfume, cosmetics, and detergents show marketing promise. They have the advantage of producing quicker results with smaller investments, less energy consumption, and less pollution. Such chemical production departments can also provide more jobs, bring in greater profits, and increase state revenues."

One of the most popular brands of Chinese-made perfume at that time was Springtime Thunder, which sold for three yuan a bottle and was every bit as potent as its name suggests. It was not long, however, before China began to advertise and sell foreign-made perfumes within China; and perfumes were not the only kinds of cosmetics that were liberated by the new policies. Foreign lipstick, eye shadow, face powder, hair dyes, and various kinds of face creams also began appearing for sale.

In April of 1981, Avon Products began producing Ai Fen Cream, or "Love Fragrance Cream," at the Beijing No. 4 Daily Needs Chemical Factory for the domestic Chinese market. Avon Products, whose cosmetics are sold in thirty-two countries by independent salespeople, had hoped to be able to bring their traditional "Avon calling," door-to-door approach to China, but the idea had to be abandoned after unsuccessful negotiations with the Chinese. As George Ittner, director of new ventures for Avon, put it, "The system wouldn't accommodate it for obvious reasons." Instead, Avon signed a coproduction contract with the China National Light Industrial Import and Export Corporation to manufacture face cream in China to American standards. One ounce of Ai Fen Cream in a white jar with a gold top costs 2.60 yuan, or about 4 per cent of the monthly salary of an average worker.

In November of 1981, three hundred cosmetics-factory "executives" convened in Peking to discuss ways of strengthening their new industry. Their final proposal called for expanding production of Chinese cosmetics at a 25 per cent annual rate for the next four years. Participants believed that this rate of growth might very well be surpassed once the "rural market" of peasants who had acquired new wealth under the responsibility system was tapped—a unique marketing strategy for Chinese manufacturers, who had historically ignored the rural peasant as too poor to bother with. Now, however, with wealth being accumulated in the countryside and a new class of rich peasants and entrepreneurs springing up as a result of the decollectivization of agriculture, some of China's executives were suddenly starting to sound like Western merchants of old dreaming of China's potentially lucrative internal markets. As Chinese peasant society began to polarize economically into classes, some of its members were in fact becoming wealthy enough to think about luxuries such as cosmetics, which had traditionally been bought only by urban Chinese. Of all the changes taking place in China, surely this was one of the most unexpected.

To their pre-existing line of cosmetics, which concentrated heavily on face powders (such as Bee and Flower Nourishing Powder and Double Happiness Pearl Frost Powder), cosmetic factory executives soon added such Western nostrums as underarm deodorant and a new depilatory cream to remove unwanted body and facial hair. The announcement of the latter created a whole series of human interest stories in the Chinese press about women who, after silently suffering for years from the affliction of unwanted body hair, had at last found a remedy.

When the cream, called Liangfu Shuang, or "Cream to Brighten the Skin," was announced as having been successfully tested, its manufacturer, the Shanghai No. 9 Pharmaceutical Company, and several drugstores in Shanghai which had been designated as outlets received over 100,000 letters of inquiry from potential consumers. According to one news account, prior to the introduction of Liangfu Shuang there had been daily lines of hirsute people outside a clinic at the Shanghai No. 1 Maternity and Children's Hospital, but that for most cases doctors had been unable to recommend an effective therapy. *China Youth News* ran an article about an old woman who, heartsick because her three daughters had thick hair on their arms and chests and were thus unable to find husbands, had come all the way from Shenyang in Manchuria to Shanghai to find a remedy, and when the depilatory cream actually went on sale, thousands of people mobbed the counters of stores in Canton which carried it in hopes of getting some. So popular and well-known did Liangfu Shuang become that the Shanghai Film Studio ultimately made a short feature about it for airing on the Central People's Television Network.

Evidently all this new interest in cosmetics was having repercussions in the workplace as well. Women, concerned with maintaining their femininity, were reportedly beginning to evade jobs that roughened or sunburned their skin or made their bodies too muscular and masculine-looking. In January, 1982, the *Liberation Daily* complained that some female workers in Shanghai had started to request transfers from physically demanding work because they had been unduly influenced by Chinese and foreign film stars, calendar girls, and cover girls on magazines. It admonished Party authorities to take account of the social consequences of magazines that lionized beautiful, fey young women who led "Westernized lives of ease and comfort."

In the early nineteen-eighties, magazines concentrating on movies, fashion, and sports had begun to reappear in China, and many were, in fact, using cover photographs of pretty young women. Even the staid *Beijing Review* appeared in July, 1984, with a full back page color ad for

Flying Pigeon bicycles which featured a lovely young woman leaning against a bike in designer jeans, with an up-to-date coiffure, and sporting a winsome smile. As early as March, 1982, the *People's Daily* published a letter from one outraged citizen who claimed to have done a survey in which he found that out of 792 magazine issues published the previous year, 218 were emblazoned with such photographs. He noted disdainfully that their only conceivable function was to titillate customers into buying the magazines, thus making money for publishing houses.

When I asked a young woman who works in the Chinese fashion industry if she felt that the way Chinese women viewed themselves had really changed profoundly over the last few years, she replied, "Women are much more vain now. It used to be that in looking for a husband a young woman would not have talked about what a boy looked like, and would have thought instead about whether or not they were politically correct, had good jobs, or had access to an apartment. But now people's looks, the shape of their body, and the kinds of clothes they wear have become just as important. And no one cares about politics."

Trying to moderate the growing amount of attention Chinese were investing in their appearance, one Shanghai paper admonished those who put fashion consciousness before work to remember that "using the sweat of one's own labor to contribute to socialist modernization truly gives expression to inner beauty." If there were many young, urban Chinese listening to this advice, it was certainly not obvious to me.

One of the most arresting changes in Chinese attitudes toward Western style, though, had nothing to do with cosmetics, clothes, or fashion. On August 10, 1981, an article in *China Sports News*, a paper that usually deals with athletics and health, sallied forth into unusual territory. "The healthy young feminine physique, rich in curves, displays the charm of youth," it said. "But some women, reaching their growth period with breasts still perfectly flat, worry about it . . . and thus psychologically it occupies a very important position [in their lives]." In previous times when politics were "in command," the shape of a woman's body was considered a forbidden subject of discussion, but now that tight-fitting Western clothes have taken hold at least in China's cities, and the traditional tight-fitting Chinese *qipao* has staged a comeback, Chinese women have once again become concerned with a good hip and bustline. And what sort of solution did *China Sport News* have in mind for flat-chested Chinese girls? It mentioned better nutrition, exercise, hormones, and even plastic surgery, although it gave no indication how widespread the latter practice might be in China. However, it was surprising, to put it mildly, simply to find the subject mentioned in the official Chinese press at all.

In June of 1984, however, Song Ruyao, director of the Plastic Surgery Hospital of the Chinese Academy of Medical Sciences and president of the Chinese Plastic Surgery Society, told the New China News Agency that with the steady increase in China's living standard, one could expect more and more demand for cosmetic surgery involving reconstruction of eyelids, noses, and breasts. He made no comment about whether or not he felt such a trend to be healthy.

The most common kind of cosmetic surgery performed in China today is surgery on the epicanthus of the eyelid, which gives the eye a rounder and more Western look by adding a second fold. "The love of beauty is human nature," Dr. Song recently told a reporter from the *China Daily*. "Now that the people's living standard has improved, and they have begun to want more from life, some girls think that single-fold eyelids are not beautiful enough." In February, 1982, when Michael Weisskopf, Peking bureau chief for the *Washington Post*, visited a clinic that performed such surgery, he found a private business run by a frail fifty-eight-year-old man with one blind eye who worked out of his own house, using his bedroom for an operating room and a reading lamp for a surgical light. Dr. Fu Lungyu, who had learned his trade as a medical student thirty years before, applied for and received a permit from the Peking municipal government to run his private business in 1981 (after the responsibility system had been implemented in China). Since then he has been modifying Chinese eyes to look more Western for forty yuan. In the fourteen months before Weisskopf visited him, he had performed six hundred operations, earning 24,000 yuan.

"A few years ago, ideological purity was the only requisite," Dr. Fu told Weisskopf between operations at his small clinic. "Now people pay as much attention to outside beauty as to inside beauty."

"I was no match for my handsome boyfriend," one young female patient who had had her eyes fixed told Weisskopf. "I wanted to catch up with him."

"My husband has been very considerate," another, older patient told him. "I wanted to show him I loved life. Life is beautiful, so people should also be."

The idea that beauty is related to looking Western was, and presumably still is, abhorrent to Maoists and even to many patriotic Chinese, many of whom have spent their whole lives struggling to disentangle China from foreign domination of all kinds. Deeply sensitive to any insinuation that China is inferior to the West, Chinese revolutionaries now confront the anomalous situation of watching their young people troop off to eye surgeons to be made to look more Western, just the way young women in American client states such as Thailand, the Philippines, Taiwan, and South Korean (not to speak of Vietnam during the war) have done for years. Such slavish imitation of things Western was exactly the kind of abasement of "Chineseness" which had proved so humiliating to the generation that made the Chinese Revolution in the first place; and in no small measure it was because of the way Chinese had felt humbled by invidious comparisons with the richer and more powerful West that Mao finally chose the path of isolation for his country. Now, when Western styles are again ascendant among urban Chinese, the voices that once cried out so insistently that China should purge itself of all forms of foreign domination are frequently muted. But it would be erronous to assume such voices no longer exist. Not only do they exist but they still represent a strong faction in China. However, being currently out of favor and thus rarely heard because they are not in control of the public media, they often appear to have been vanquished. Nonetheless, from time to time they manage to speak out, rising like a dissonant chord above an otherwise carefully arranged musical score. At such times we are, for a fleeting moment, reminded that even though China is a dictatorship, unanimity among the Chinese leadership and the 40 million members of the Chinese Communist Party is actually far from complete.

One of the most common targets of criticism for these neo-Maoists is China's youth and the way they have been affected by Deng's open-door policy. For instance, in the spring of 1979, Peking Radio broadcast an attack on the "unhealthy trends" it saw emerging among students, such as the wearing of long hair, bell-bottom pants, and lipstick, as well as "billing and cooing" in public places. *China Youth News* came quickly to the defense of these young people. It acknowledged that youth should indeed work and study diligently, but it did not agree that it was "necessary to force everyone to lead the same way of life." The article went on to say: "It is further inadvisable to confuse a love of ordinary life with ideology. Hair and bell-bottom trousers have no connection with good or bad ideological thinking." Broadening its defense, *China Youth News* reminded its readers that many currently accepted Chinese styles, such as crew-cuts and trousers of any kind, had originally been adopted from Western countries, and asked if those who opposed Western fashions now would have Chinese return to wearing robes and pantaloons.

Such rejoinders did little, however, to still the fears of those—some of whom were high within the Chinese Communist Party—who believed that China's revolutionary essence was being corrupted by Western influences and who rejected the notion that the best of Western capitalist systems could be borrowed and applied in socialist China, while the rest could be neatly pared away and discarded. For these Chinese, a dichotomy like that between *ti* and *yong*, or "essence" and "function," was dangerous, because they believed that the adoption of Western *yong*, or practical things like technology, led inevitably to a contamination of Chinese *ti*, or essence. For them, there seemed to be no middle ground. But what was China to do? Close its doors, sink once again into isolation, and lose its momentum to modernize? Some doubtless thought such a path preferable to the current alternative, and over the next few years they would not miss a chance to press their attack against such obvious signs of "degenerate" behavior as youth fashions.

For instance, in October, 1981, Liaoning Provincial Radio in Manchuria broadcast a news item about a proclamation issued by a group of municipal organizations that apparently shared this point of view. The proclamation urged young people "not to wear weird clothes or their hair long, and not to dance rock-and-roll in order to improve social habits." It also urged them not to wear bell-bottom pants or "crosses" (crucifixes), and exhorted boys "not to wear feminine clothing, high-heeled shoes, or queer-looking hats, and not to wear their hair in weird long styles. . . . Whistling, shouting, making trouble, and saying vulgar words at recreation spots, including cinemas, theaters, and stadiums, are discouraged. Youths are urged not to drink wine, nor to fight, nor to crowd around foreigners and overseas Chinese compatriots at public places."

In February, 1982, the *Beijing Daily* published an article similarly critical of youth culture. While agreeing that such things as styles of dress and makeup were highly personal choices, it claimed that some young Chinese "do not understand what true beauty is . . . , blindly worship bourgeois lifestyles, see 'foreign' as 'beautiful' and their own nation's beauty as 'ugly.' " It went on to warn young Chinese men that in the West such affectations as long or wavy hair were adopted mainly by "spiritually barren" men. In a Western country such official admonitions against certain kinds of behavior could be taken at face value, but in China, where massive political campaigns have often grown out of small, seemingly innocuous criticisms, the mere mention in a negative tone of something like bell-bottom pants or long hair is enough to send a signal all across China that larger, more important issues probably lie beneath the surface.

This ongoing and, at times, seemingly schizophrenic debate over life-styles continued for the next few years in a desultory fashion. It was not until 1983 that it kindled into a major controversy in which one could see that behind the façade of unity in Deng's new China serious disagreements still existed on how China should go about modernizing and dealing with Western influence. At that time two significant movements began: one, to "rectify" the Party of members who harbored ideologically impure thoughts—namely, "unreconstructed leftists," or Maoists; and the other, to purge the masses of "spiritual pollution," which was defined as "unhealthy" bourgeois and foreign influences. Fashion, being at once so ephemeral and so obviously inspired by Western culture (in comparison with science and technology —which were also borrowed, but more neutral and clearly more functional), became an obvious symbolic target for those who actually opposed the whole thrust of Deng's overall reforms.

Curiously, it was Deng himself who launched the anti-spiritual pollution campaign at the Second Plenum of the Twelfth Central Committee on October 11, 1983, by defining "spiritual pollution" as "disseminating all varieties of corrupt and decadent ideologies of the burgeoise and other exploiting classes, and disseminating sentiments of distrust toward the socialist and communist cause and the Communist Party leadership."

Thomas Gold, a professor of sociology at the University

of California, Berkeley, and a keen observer of the Chinese youth movement, has called Deng's public support for the campaign "a tactical feint against the right in order to garner support from the Party's left for the impending rectification" of the Party membership. In other words, Deng hoped to mollify the neo-Maoists, who felt that the new open-door policy had allowed too much uncontrolled Western influence, with a well-controlled assault on "spiritual pollution." In return, Deng hoped to get them to go along with his housecleaning of the Party. He was very careful, however, to draw distinctions between what he called a "drive" against spiritual pollution and the larger political "campaigns" that had so disruptively seized China during the Cultural Revolution. He must have been well aware that those who opposed his policies of economic liberalization and of opening China to the outside world would have liked nothing better than to use a new "political campaign" to rid the country both of his own leadership and of the heterodox influences that had swept in from abroad over the previous few years. In fact, there is every evidence that this is exactly what they tried covertly to do once the "drive" against spiritual pollution got going.

Deng Liqun, the Party's propaganda chief and one of the "drive's" strongest supporters, defined what he considered the four main kinds of spiritual pollution to be: namely, spreading things that are "obscene, barbarous, treacherous, or reactionary; vulgar taste in artistic performances; efforts to seek personal gain and indulgence in individualism, anarchism, and liberalism; writing articles or delivering speeches that run counter to the country's social system."

Taking their cue from the Second Plenum, many Chinese papers suddenly began, in the fall of 1983, to publish commentories and articles about the need to combat spiritual pollution. Leaders such as President Li Xiannian spoke of the necessity for the working class to "resist and overcome all forms of spiritual pollution," as if the affliction were caused by an invading army of microbes that could be beaten back by good hygiene. On October 23, the *People's Daily* published an article criticizing intellectuals whose thinking and writing had led to a "mistrust of socialism." It was echoed on October 24, when the *Guangming Daily*, a leading intellectual newspaper in Peking, denounced those Chinese who had become uncritically accepting of Western art and literature: "They deny the basic distinction between capitalist literature and art, and socialist literature and art, corrupting us and making inroads." While the paper defended the exchange of foreign science, technology, management, and equipment, it balked at the idea of uncontrolled cultural exchanges, saying: "There exist foreign bourgeois elements with hopes of using these exchanges to seek 'those with different political views' and 'undemocratic individualists' here, to influence our country to shake off rule by 'socialist dictatorship' and follow a 'liberal path.' "

On October 31, Minister of Culture Zhu Muzhi cautioned Chinese in an article in the *People's Daily* that spiritual pollution was not only a problem among intellectuals and in Marxist theory, but that it had also sprung up in "performances that propagandized for violent things that were depraved and sexual in nature, and in stinking bourgeois life-styles dedicated to nothing more than having a good time, drinking, resting, and hedonism." The same day, veteran revolutionary writer Ding Ling chimed in, also in the *People's Daily*, lamenting: "It's gotten to the point that when someone sings 'Without the Communist Party There Would Be No China,' people laugh derisively. Another peculiar thing is that, because some foreign scholars praise certain works, our people say they are good."

Joining the "drive," the Peking Municipal Government suddenly issued a new dress code for its staff, prohibiting its female employees from wearing "unwholesome" ornaments, hair that came below the shoulders, and too many cosmetics. Men were forbidden to wear long hair, mustaches, beards, and sideburns. "We must preserve our habits of simplicity and bitter struggle," the *Beijing Daily* said in explaining the new regulations. "Hats and clothing must be clean and simple. Bizarre dress is forbidden."

As part of the campaign, the Xidan Department Store in Peking required seventy of its young staff members to get rid of "strange" hairstyles, and made more than twenty saleswomen stop wearing earrings, eye makeup, and lipstick. The Central College of Arts and Crafts in Peking announced that it would require all students who had "long and strange" hairstyles to have haircuts as a condition for registration. To facilitate this ritual of purification, the school administration set up a barber next door to the registrar's office. Universities and youth organizations throughout China held mass meetings to warn against the dangers of spiritual pollution. Party leaders even claimed to have encountered signs of spiritual pollution in Tibet. By November, two high-ranking staff members of the *People's Daily*, Hu Jiwei, the director, and Wang Roushi, the deputy editor-in-chief, had been dismissed for not embracing the purification movement with sufficient editorial ardor.

Of course, not even the staunchest supporters of the movement could ever come right out and themselves attack the policies that were presumably leading to all this "spiritual pollution"—namely, Deng Xiaoping's "open door" and such new economic innovations as the responsibility system. This would have put them in direct opposition to the ruling faction. Even Deng Liqun himself was forced to voice at least *pro forma* support for the open-door policy and to stress that China's leaders were not about to allow a runaway political campaign against Westernization to develop.

Nonetheless, the movement caused ordinary citizens all across China to grow apprehensive about becoming too closely identified with things Western or bourgeois. Young people became less conspicuous in their style of dress. Intellectuals began to clam up and avoid contact with foreigners. Workers grew wary of buying too many ostentatious material goods. Peasants pulled back from engaging in business that might leave them exposed to charges of taking the "capitalist road." People feared that a major anti-rightist campaign might be brewing, and that the preceding period of liberalization might turn out to be just a ruse, which in the words of Mao after a similar period of liberalization in the 1950s, could be used to lure "the demons and hobgoblins to come out of their lairs in order to wipe them out better, and [to] let the seeds sprout to make it more convenient to hoe them." In short, much of the energy for modernization—which relied on private capitalistic initiative as well as foreign capital and technology—disappeared, as people everywhere drew back to protect themselves against the possibility of a new wave of ultra-leftism.

This was too much for Deng, who, though involved in complicated factional struggles, was still in control of both the Party and the military. The brakes were quickly put on the anti-spiritual-pollution movement. On November 17, 1983, a commentary from *China Youth News*, reprinted in the *People's Daily*, and entitled "Pollution Should Be Eliminated but Life Should Be Beautified," claimed that victims of spiritual pollution should be viewed as "comrades" in need of reform rather than as "criminals," and that makeup, high heels, and bell-bottom pants should not be mistaken for signs of spiritual pollution. Speaking of youth's new interest in fashion, the editorial said: "We must not criticize the young for appreciating stylish clothes and good food and for having fun. We must not attach importance to the shape of pants, to the height of shoe heels, or to hairdos, but instead we should defend and back the legitimate aspirations of the young who want to embellish their lives. In some areas comrades have attacked girls who wear makeup and go for a perm, they ban the young from sporting stylish clothes and from indulging in healthy dancing, and even go so far as to frown on growing flowers." The editorial concluded by saying that the Party should spell out a "clear line of demarcation between the embellishments of life and spiritual pollution."

After this, the Party let it be known loud and clear that the anti-spiritual-pollution campaign would not be allowed to affect religion, science, and technology *or* the booming rural economy where peasants had been showing signs of growing restive about what was happening. These reassurances signalled the effective end of the campaign. On December 21, an article in the *People's Daily* made it clear that the campaign had gone too far and should be curtailed: "What is worth paying attention to now is that some have expanded the elimination of spiritual pollution into daily life. This is wrong. People should not mix up spiritual pollution with changes in material and cultural life; even more, they should not interfere excessively with different customs of life."

In a note from the editor entitled "Ideological Contamination Clarified," the *Beijing Review*'s political editor, An Zhiguo, wrote in February, 1984, that "opinions differed as to what the term 'ideological contamination' implied," and that the Party needed to clarify "the confusion and oversensitiveness spreading among many people." He maintained that such ideological contamination referred only to "erroneous words and actions that deviate from Marxism and socialism, decadent ideas such as pursuing profit as one's only aim and the influence of pornography. In short, it is limited to the ideological sphere, and has nothing to do with science and economics."

And what of fashion? "Over the last few years people have become increasingly fashion conscious," An acknowledged. ". . . This should not be regarded as ideological contamination; rather, people should be encouraged to wear beautiful clothes and enliven their daily activities."

An spoke of the need to oppose "left" and "feudal" trends "which cannot even tolerate descriptions of love in literature and art, and which label 'obscene' any television or movie scenes showing men and women kissing and embracing." He went on to say, "We offer no objections to paintings and sculptures that depict the beauty of the human body, and still less do we oppose efforts to draw on the strength of outstanding Western works of art." These were surprising words from an official Chinese publication, ones well calculated to reassure nervous Chinese that there would be no new political campaign, and that "no overbearing steps will be taken against those holding different views."

By the spring, things had begun to return to the *status quo ante*. For instance, the sale of cosmetics was booming once again. The People's Market in Nanjing reported that during the first three months of 1984 it had sold 170,000 yuan worth of cosmetics such as lipstick, rouge, and nail polish. Newspapers reported that at some large stores in Canton, far from forbidding saleswomen to wear cosmetics, management was actually encouraging them to put on makeup as "an outward sign of respect for their customers," as one writer put it.

By April, 1984, one heard very little about the dangers of spiritual pollution. Deng Liqun had reportedly been eased from office. Reagan was in China—which he referred to as the "so-called Communist China"—promoting "friendship" and paving the way for an even greater exchange of trade, finance, technology, culture, and arms. China's door to the outside was open wider than ever, fears about contamination by bourgeois values notwithstanding.

During the summer of 1984, for instance, I received a letter from a Chinese friend in Peking, who had recently graduated from the Fashion Institute of Technology in New York City and was setting up a company to export her own designer clothing from China to the United States, "Living here in Peking for almost three months now after New York, I cannot help but feel how much things have changed," she wrote. "The young people are so bold and fearless in dressing themselves up in modern Western clothes that I think it will not take much more Western influence before they will be able to accept high fashion from Paris."

The latest campaign against spiritual pollution was

clearly over, but it was still evident that China's ambivalence about being Westernized was far from resolved. Although critics of Westernization at least momentarily fell silent, few Chinese I met believed that they had actually disappeared. The campaign against spiritual pollution had made it clear to all that those forces that opposed Deng Xiaoping's open-door policy were still ones to be reckoned with. Minimally, this brief movement was a warning to everyone that even while "modernizing," China still had socialist pretensions, and that the new freedoms were not without limits even though at times these limits might be difficult to pinpoint.

As the authors of *Intellectual Freedom in China After Mao*, an informative report written in 1984 by Liang Heng and Judith Shapiro for the Fund for Free Expression (which keeps account of the state of human rights in a whole variety of countries), noted, the campaign against spiritual pollution "sharply reminded [Chinese] that their main task was the inculcation of socialist values and enthusiasm for the socialist cause, and that those who hoped to investigate the roots of society's ills, express their own inner worlds, or espouse humanistic concern for others were given a clear message to be silent."

★

One day in 1984, while flying to Canton (Guangzhou) from Shanghai on a Chinese plane, I picked up the new in-flight magazine of the Civil Aviation Administration of China (CAAC), and was stunned to see on its back cover a full-page glossy color advertisement for Yves Saint-Laurent's Opium perfume. I had been surprised many times by what I had found in China since Deng Xiaoping opened the door to the West, but nothing could have prepared me for this bizarre manifestation of his new policies. Opium had, of course, been the original source of contention between China and the

Western powers in the eighteenth and nineteenth centuries, when, in contravention of Chinese law, English, American, and other Western merchants, supported by their respective governments, had imported large amounts of the drug into China and traded it at enormous profit for silk, tea, and silver.

If any single historical incident might be said to epitomize Western imperialist aggression in China as well as the legacy of inequality and bitterness that ensued, it was surely the Opium Wars that followed Chinese efforts in 1839 to confiscate and burn 20,000 chests of English opium stored in Canton. The British reacted angrily by sending an expeditionary naval force to China which proceeded to launch attacks all the way up the China coast to Tientsin. When the defeated Chinese finally signed the humiliating Treaty of Nanking in 1842, they were not only forced to cede Hong Kong to the British and to open up five coastal "treaty ports" (Canton, Amoy, Foochow, Ningpo, and Shanghai) to foreign residence and trade, but also to pay a large indemnity to Britain to reimburse English merchants for their confiscated opium.

Even had I not come across the Yves Saint-Laurent ad, going to Canton is always a jarring reminder of China's embattled past and its long and unequal relationship with the West. For it was from Canton that Western merchants first penetrated China. It was from here in the aftermath of the Opium Wars that the humiliating "unequal treaties" spread the treaty ports northward, giving foreign traders, missionaries, and soldiers the right to live and work in China and yet be exempt from almost every aspect of Chinese life, including the law. It was from the Canton area that hundreds of thousands of Chinese "coolies" (from the Chinese *kuli*, meaning "bitter labor") emigrated to the North American West Coast to work in the gold mines and build the railroads during the middle of the last century. It was here that Sun Yat-sen and China's Republican Revolution against the last imperial dynasty found such fertile soil at the turn of the century. It was here also that Chiang Kai-shek retreated in 1949, with the embassies of those countries that recognized him until the bitter end, just before Mao's armies swept down from the north and finally drove him off the Chinese mainland to Taiwan.

In short, Guangdong province has almost always been at the cutting edge of China's relations with the West, sharing borders as it does with the English and Portuguese colonies of Hong Kong and Macao. Perhaps, then, it is hardly surprising to find that during this most recent transformation of China, Canton, the province's capital, is once again in the forefront of change, and that free enterprise and foreign influence have reached their most extreme expression there to date.

As one moves nearer to the city of Canton, one feels the increasing force of Western influence radiating outward from the two colonies, just as one can feel the growing intensity of heat as one approaches an open fire. In contrast to North China, from which relatively few people have emigrated to other countries, almost every other person in Guangdong has some relative who lives abroad. Such familial ties have formed a powerful historical connection between these southern Chinese and the outside world; and now that China has abandoned the kind of class politics that once pitted rich against poor, and revolutionary China against the reactionary countries of the outside capitalist world, visas are easy to procure and a tidal wave of overseas Chinese have begun making pilgrimages back to Guangdong to re-establish ties with their "old homes" (*laojia*).

The trains, boats, and planes coming into Guangdong from Hong Kong and Macao are filled with overseas Chinese loaded down with electronic appliances, shopping bags full of liquor, cigarettes, video cassettes, clothing, and other luxury items not available in China. They wear the latest Western fashions, makeup, and hairstyles, and have about them a brusque, businesslike air that unmis-

takably differentiates them from their Chinese relatives
who wait eagerly for them and their booty at stations,
docks, and airports inside China. Not only are these overseas relatives apostles of a very different way of life (coming from as far away as the United States, Canada, South-
east Asia, and Europe), but many of them have become
wealthy since their departure from their homeland; and
since foreign investment laws in China have recently
changed—particularly with regard to overseas "compatriots"—these Chinese have begun to pump enormous sums
of money back into Guangdong.

In March, 1984, at the third anniversary meeting of the
Guangdong International Trust and Investment Corporation (attended by representatives of 375 companies and of
49 banking groups from Hong Kong and Macao), Provincial
Governor Liang Lingguang reported that between 1978 and
1983, 32,000 contracts worth $4.6 billion U.S. had been
signed between foreign and Guangdong business concerns. In
1983 alone, Liang told the meeting, the number of signed
contracts had increased by 32 per cent. These figures do
not include the millions of dollars of foreign currency remitted each year to Chinese in Guangdong by overseas relatives as gifts, loans, or informal investments that are being
used to start up many of the small-scale private businesses
now springing up all around the Pearl River Delta, creating
an enormous economic boom. As an article in the June 4,
1984 *Beijing Review* candidly put it: "The new boom is
attributable to the area's favorable climate, proximity to
Hong Kong and Macao, and most important, the implemen-
tation of the central authorities' special policies for opening Guangdong and other coastal provinces and cities to
the outside world."

Guangdong province is also the location of three of
China's four Special Economic Zones, which the government
authorized in 1979 to lure foreign investment and new industry not then permitted in the rest of the country into
China with promises of income tax holidays, exemptions on

both import and export customs duties, low rents and wages, and the possibility of important new domestic Chinese markets. The three Guangdong Special Economic Zones, all ports, are located in Shenzhen, just across the border from Hong Kong; Zuhai, just across the border from Macao; and Shantou (once called Swatow), up the Guangdong coast to the north.

The idea of these zones is twofold—not only to attract foreign investment and technology to China but also to cordon off pockets of concentrated foreign intrusion so that the rest of China will not be spiritually polluted by them. In the case of Shenzhen, the largest and most developed Special Economic Zone, the Chinese government budgeted $70 million to build a high barbed-wire fence around the entire 127-square-mile zone. The notion was a naive one, since Shenzhen, which five years ago was a small rural town of 30,000 people, had by 1984 grown into an uncontainable boomtown with a population of more than 300,000, 370 factories, an annual industrial output of more than 673 million yuan, and a work force of thousands who go back and forth across the border from China proper to work each day. It also harbored China's first department store selling foreign consumer goods to Chinese, a resort (the Honey Lake Country Club), China's first eighteen-hole golf course, a French ocean liner converted into a 235-room luxury hotel, an amusement park with sixty-two entertainment devices imported from Japan and Italy (including a huge roller coaster), a television broadcasting station, a new railroad station, and (under construction) a $3 billion, six-lane superhighway that will connect the zone to Hong Kong and Canton, a fifty-two-story hotel (which will be the highest building in China), as well as sixty other buildings over eighteen floors high. By 1984, the average annual per capita income of zone workers was 1,500 yuan, approximately five times the national average; one-fifth of the local peasant families were reported by the Chinese press to have attained the exalted status of "ten-thousand-yuan households"; and the zone itself had concluded 2,500 contracts and agreements with foreign business people, drawing $1.8 billion in foreign investments.

Visually, the Special Economic Zones are vast, dusty, sprawling expanses of land littered with construction materials and reverberating with the sounds of bulldozers, trucks, and pile drivers. As in so many past projects, once the Chinese make a decision to do something, they go at it with a determination and haste that are often astounding, and equally disastrous because they so frequently lead to poor planning and sloppy construction. Being in a Special Economic Zone, one cannot help but feel the intensity of the energy, but it is an energy which, although aimed in a decidedly capitalistic direction, is in many ways reminiscent of Mao's Revolution, when the fury of the moment gripped everyone, causing them to rush forward with an invincible but often reckless optimism and speed. China is no longer building backyard steel mills, or using thousands of people with baskets and carrying poles to build dams and dikes, following hastily contrived plans to make the Communist Revolution incarnate. But, with the same hellbent energy and impatience, they have now set about constructing a new answer to China's woes: the Special Economic Zone, designed to link China to the wealth and power of the West and serve as a new type of catalyst for China's deliverance from backwardness.

At the end of January, 1984, just as the campaign against spiritual pollution was being terminated, Deng Xiaoping himself made a tour of the Special Economic Zones. So convinced did he become of the zones' correctness and efficacy that upon returning to Peking, he proposed to the Secretariat of the Chinese Communist Party Central Committee that the special status granted to the zones be extended to other ports as well. In April, the government announced that fourteen new coastal cities, from Hainan Island in the south to Dalian in the north, would be opened and granted similar status, so that "the vitality of foreign economic relations" could be spread.

Not since the old treaty ports had China seen such an extensive network of coastal entrepôts open to foreigners; and not only was China geographically expanding the areas open to investment, it was also making the terms of investment more and more enticing. For the first time foreigners were allowed to establish "exclusive" (or 100 per cent) investments, which did away with the old restrictions requiring that the Chinese maintain a majority share in every foreign company investing in China as they had in the cases of the Jianguo and Great Wall hotels. If a foreign investment was to be of a high-tech nature, or if it was more than $30 million, the foreign company involved would be allowed duty-free imports, and be accorded preferential income-tax rates as well as the right to sell a portion of their goods on the local market.

Chinese leaders seemed less and less concerned about the kind of restrictive but protective regulations that had once been a hallmark of their country's militantly independent policy. "The expansion of the open [door] policy does not mean that China will change its principles of independence and self-reliance," wrote Jin Qi, economic editor of the *Beijing Review* in May, 1984, evincing sensitivity to insinuations that China might be abandoning its former commitment to stand on its own feet. "The foreign funds and advanced technology we import," he went on, "in accordance with the principles of equality and mutual benefit, will be used to expedite our domestic economic development and increase our self-reliance." This new flexibility sent off a scramble among the new ports for foreign capital. Local leaders started vying with each other in a competitive fashion unknown in China for decades. They gave interviews and ran ads in the English-language *China Daily*, extolling the climate for investment in their particular areas. HAINAN, "PROFITABLE" HAVEN FOR INVESTORS read the headline for one article in which Lei Yu, director of the Hainan Prefecture Administration, boasted that "foreign investors can expect to make more profits on Hainan Island than in many other parts of China." TIANJING OPENS INVESTOR ZONE broadcast the headline to another article, in which the vice-mayor of Tianjing, Li Lanqing, announced that his city would offer special tax advantages to foreigners, build a new telephone system, and open six new hotels all managed by foreigners for the convenience of overseas businessmen. He also reminded potential investors that, unlike before, his municipal government was now empowered to approve foreign projects involving investments of up to $30 million without having to seek permission from Peking. This was a significant development that suggested yet another radical change. By decentralizing decision-making power and allowing so many new cities and localities to deal directly with foreign businessmen, the Chinese government was in effect promoting regionalism. Almost immediately the competition among these various regional centers escalated further.

By the middle of 1984, inland cities were also being granted new authority to deal directly with foreign investors, rather than having to go through the appropriate ministry in Peking.

Suddenly, every city of consequence in China was holding investment seminars and inviting businessmen from around the world to attend. In April, 1984, officials in the Peking municipal government announced that they were searching out $150 million in foreign capital to develop 120 key industries. They noted that they would entertain offers from foreign businessmen for joint, as well as exclusive, ventures.

The same month, Shanxi province held a symposium with foreign businessmen at which contracts for $20 million were signed with overseas firms. In June, Hubei province, Central China's largest industrial area, held a conference in Wuhan, the provincial capital, to which foreign businessmen from all over the world were invited, the purpose being to explore the possibilities of their becoming involved in one hundred different local projects. The conference was part of Hubei's effort to find $1 billion U.S. to modernize two thousand of its key enterprises over the next decade and a half.

Even the remote Ningxia Hui Autonomous Region, a minority area in the desolate, landlocked Northwest of China, announced it would hold an "international symposium," and that all foreign joint ventures would be accorded a complete exemption from taxes for the first five years of profit, followed by a second five-year grace period with a 50 per cent tax reduction.

Whatever concern China's leaders might have evinced for the notion of "self-reliance" in past years now seemed to have been eclipsed by the mad rush for foreign investment. There were few cautionary notes about the danger of China once again becoming overly dependent on foreign investment and technology in this fever to open the door to the outside wider and wider. Few Chinese seemed mindful of the dismal historical record China had when, in the past, it had tried to import whole factories and systems into the country, only to see them languish because of inadequate training of Chinese workers, lack of power, poor transportation facilities, backward management, and an unreliable supply of raw materials. China had already experienced one painful postrevolutionary dependency of this nature in the nineteen-fifties, when Mao, deciding "to lean to one side," had relied exclusively on the help of Russia, China's "Soviet big brother," only to be left perilously close to collapse when Khrushchev pulled out all Soviet advisers and cancelled all aid programs in 1959.

As foreign investment poured back into China, this time from the other side of the Cold War divide, the Chinese government sought to allay the fears of foreign businessmen of another leftist revival. "The lawful rights and interests of foreign enterprises and investors will be protected by Chinese law. There is no need for them to worry about the political environment," promised Gu Ming, deputy secretary of the State Council in June, 1984." Some foreign businessmen are worried that China will nationalize or requisition their investment and property in China. There is . . . no need to worry about that," he said. Only occasionally within China would some muffled complaints surface about the way the Chinese were being seduced by the West, or the way they were giving themselves over to the quest for profits. One heard some people speak in a derogatory fashion about how most Chinese now "looked toward money as if it were everything" (*xiang qian kan*) ; or from time to time an item would come up in the press in which revulsion was expressed at how money-minded some Chinese were becoming under the new policies, only to be dismissed as wrong-thinking. For instance, an article in the China Daily on May 8, 1984, reported that officials in the Shekou section of the Shenzhen Special Economic Zone had angered some Chinese when they publicly posted a sign reading TIME IS MONEY AND EFFICIENCY IS LIFE. " 'Time is money' sounded capitalist to some people who rejected the notion that the slogan best characterized the high-speed development of the industrial zone," said the article. Dismissing such concerns, it went on to note that Deng Xiaoping had himself finally approved the disputed slogan, signalling newspapers all over China to urge other industries to adopt it.

On one of my recent trips to Guangdong province, I entered by hydrofoil through the river port of Jiangmen from Hong Kong. After we disembarked, almost the first person I saw was a dapper young Chinese man wearing a gray three-piece suit, Western tie, and well-shined shoes. He held a slender, hand-tooled leather attaché case. Assuming that he was an overseas Chinese on his way back to Hong Kong, I gave him no more thought until a few minutes later when he walked up and introduced himself in good English as Sterling Wu (a pseudonym), a guide for the China Travel Service. He was there to take our small group to Taishan county, several hours away by car. Wu, it turned out, had never been abroad, even to Hong Kong. His masterful job of replicating Western style was done completely on the basis of what he had seen and learned of the outside world within China.

The second Chinese I met also spoke English, if haltingly, and wore a Western suit, though one that was dusty and rumpled. He was also drunk. Just as I left the customs house, he approached on wobbly legs, wearing a loony smile. With his hand outstretched in greeting, he launched immediately into a confusing discussion of British actions in Guangdong during the Opium Wars. "You British weren't fair," he told me. "You came here, right here to our country, with cannons! And we . . . we couldn't . . ." Here he faded out like a radio with no antenna. In the past such a blemish on the socialist escutcheon would have been whisked off the street by Security Bureau police long before any foreigner had had a chance to see him, let alone be subjected to the beginning of an inebriated history lesson. But now there were so many foreigners in China, and the myth of socialist perfection had been punctured so thoroughly, that no one paid heed to him.

Leaving the dock area, Sterling Wu took us for lunch at what was apparently Jiangmen's newest and probably best hotel—the East Lake Guest House. Built with overseas Chinese capital, this curiously awkward-looking structure combined the worst of Eastern and Western architecture. Outside was a fish pond set in a bamboo grove in a suggestively Oriental manner, but stepping over the threshold into the lobby, one entered an entirely different ambience. A tape of country-and-Western singer Conway Twitty was being played over a sound system. Crystal chandeliers, looking as out of place as a Shang dynasty bronze in a truck stop, hung in the dining room, which was divided with folding partitions covered with rubberized floral-print wallpaper. The waitresses wore uniforms topped with bright red vests that matched the tablecloths. At first glance, the room appeared to be a perfect, if bizarre, reincarnation of Ramada Inn modernity here in Guangdong; but as I sat down to absorb my surroundings in greater detail, I began to notice flaws and to realize that what I was looking at was an illusion. There were flies buzzing in the air. The table-cloths were splotched with soy sauce and food stains. The waitresses' uniforms were soiled, their service lackadaisical. The wall-to-wall carpeting was covered with big greasy stains and was bisected by a dark trail of wetness that led from the rest rooms, which, though recently constructed, were already dirty and falling apart. The East Lake Guest House, on a second look, only underscored the difficulty the Chinese were having in successfully imitating the West.

While Mao's political ideology still held sway, a Western visitor had no more expectation of finding a Western-style restaurant in a country town like Jiangmen—or even in Peking or Shanghai—than a store that took credit cards or a café where one could sit down quietly with a friend and have a cup of good coffee. Credit cards and coffee were not "Chinese," and China was not about to swerve out of its revolutionary orbit to provide them for foreigners. While refusals to accommodate such foreign habits were perhaps inconvenient, they did imbue China with a uniqueness that made visits there seem exotic and exciting. Unlike so many other countries a traveller might visit, China could make a visitor feel utterly lost to the outside world. A trip there was more of an escape than a journey to the remotest mountain or jungle regions of Africa or South America. The gravita-tional pull of China's own special brand of politics had a way of making Westerners feel that once they were across the border, they had embarked on the ultimate form of travel in which nothing would give them that sudden half-jarring, half-soothing sense of familiarity.

How starkly the situation had actually changed was brought home to me one afternoon in Taicheng, the county seat of Taishan county in Guangdong. I was strolling with an American friend through a street market where peasants were buying and selling live chickens, ducks, and geese when I thought I saw a sign that said COFFEE SHOP hanging from a distant building. Drawing nearer, half disbelieving, I saw that there was indeed a small blue hand-painted placard and that it did in fact say COFFEE SHOP in English. In a moment, I heard the strains of Boy George and his Culture Club blasting out of the doorway: "Do you really want to hurt me, Do you really want to make me cry . . ." Inside I found a small, tidy, privately run snack bar with two tables. The walls were plastered with Viceroy, Coca-Cola, and Fanta decals. A Schweppes Tonic poster was pasted on the front of a glass case full of imported Hilton and Marlboro cigarettes. Above a small counter hung a menu, hand-lettered in English, saying, "Western Snacks," and offering lunch-meat, peanut-butter, and cheese sandwiches. The owner, a pleasant young man, informed us that he had relatives in Hong Kong who had bankrolled his business and kept him supplied with Western snack food. When I ordered coffee, he took a king-sized jar of Nescafé Instant off the shelf, put a teaspoonful into each of two cups, added some sweetened condensed milk, and then poured in hot water from a thermos. As I sat down with my friend to enjoy this afternoon cup of coffee, it occurred to me there was something distinctly historic about finding coffee and contemporary popular music in rural China—although Taishan was an area with much overseas Chinese contact. After so many years of defiant resistance to Western cultural and commercial intrusion, here at least the old struggle had clearly been abandoned.

In fact, as I later discovered, coffee shops have also begun opening up in Shanghai, a city that has historically been in the avant-garde of Chinese trends. Although their coffee was as undrinkable as any I have ever tasted, these new Shanghai cafés were becoming the rage of urban youth. The situation reminded me of Taipei in Taiwan when I was a student there in the early sixties, and Western affectations like coffee were just beginning to take hold. Now one can get some of the best coffee in the world in Taipei's thousands of new cafés. Was this also the future of China?

While travelling by bus from Taishan to Canton, we stopped for lunch in the city of Foshan, where the renowned Zhumiao (or Ancestral) Taoist Temple, built during the Ming dynasty, is located. Opposite the Overseas Chinese Mansion, where we ate lunch, I noticed a one-story building with a doorway through which a steady flow of young boys was passing. Walking over, I discovered that the building housed a privately run video-games parlor. Inside were ten electronic machines, blinking, burping, and bleeping, surrounded by twenty or thirty Chinese in their early teens.

An article in a newspaper recounted how Foshan was also blazing the way forward with new kinds of financial arrangements. It reported that a new, collectively run company had succeeded in getting city approval to raise five million yuan to build a cold-storage facility, warehouse, and shopping center by selling shares of stock to private investors.

Then in July, 1984, another group, the Foshan Trust and Investment Corporation, announced that it was making an $8.8 million stock offering on the public market to raise money for the construction of several power plants and textile factories. "Our announcement has shocked the country," Cai Bingyong, one of the trust's deputy general managers, told a *Wall Street Journal* writer, as thousands of Chinese stampeded to buy the securities. So successful was the trust in selling the new stock that it quickly increased their target of revenue from $8.8 to $43.9 million.

In June of 1984, Sheng Mujie, a member of the China Finance and Banking Society and deputy chief of the Shanghai Finance Research Institute, went on record as urging that stocks and bonds, absent from China since the Communist takeover in 1949, once again be used throughout the country as a means "to serve China's socialist modernization." According to Sheng, the managers of China's new privately and collectively financed enterprises, foreign joint ventures, and semi-autonomous state-run enterprises were searching desperately for new ways to raise capital. Shanghai, in his view, was an ideal place to experiment with a stocks-and-bonds market as a solution, since the first stock exchange run by Chinese had been set up there in 1919. The image of a Chinese stock market, where securities could be publicly bought and sold by foreigners as well as Chinese, was an arresting one, especially for a city that had been the stronghold of the Gang of Four and the cradle of some of the Cultural Revolution's most militant factions. "Technically there should be no problems," he confidently told a *China Daily* reporter. "Shanghai's strong industry provides a suitable background for such an experiment."

In many respects, with its particular openness to Western influences, Guangdong was even more "suitable" than Shanghai for such an experiment; for everywhere I went in the province I found evidence that the values which had previously characterized the Chinese Revolution were fast breaking down. One of the most obvious signs of this change could be seen in the attitude of Guangdong Chinese toward consumer goods. In the past, economic development policies had slighted the manufacture of such goods and light industry in favor of investment in heavy industry and agriculture. Under the new economic policies of Deng Xiaoping, however, these priorities were in the process of being reversed in an effort to show the Chinese people that there were indeed some material benefits to be gained after all the years of sacrifice for the Revolution. "For under socialism, no less than under capitalism, what can be better wished for than a billion customers willing and with the means to buy," wrote a commentator in a July, 1984, issue of the *China Daily*. For the first time in Chinese Communist history, new classes of Chinese have joined the consumer society. Homes where radios, bicycles, and wrist watches had been considered luxury items a few years ago now aspire to color television sets, radio–cassette players, refrigerators, and washing machines. Although such goods are manufactured in China, the craftsmanship is often inferior, so people prefer foreign appliances. As in the days before the Revolution, when the word *yang*, or "foreign," appended to an item was the hallmark of quality, once again China has begun to worship goods made abroad.

One chain of stores in China that sells certain foreign-made products, as well as the highest-quality domestic products, is the Friendship Stores. They were originally set up in most large cities exclusively for the use of foreign residents and visitors. All purchases had to be made with hard-currency certificates, which the government issued only to foreigners in exchange for dollars, marks, pounds, or yen. During the Maoist phases of the Revolution, these Friendship Stores were uninviting affairs located in dark, Soviet-style buildings. Since there were few "foreign friends" in China at that time aside from the diplomatic community, a sprinkling of tourists, and a few expatriates and members of the press, the stores were usually quite empty. Shopping in a Friendship Store was a depressing experience. There were no bargains. Little attempt was made to brighten them up. Obviously bored clerks in their Mao suits stared into space, unconcerned about whether or not they made sales. Security guards stood watch at the front doors to turn back any local Chinese indiscreet enough to try to enter. (One Chinese friend of mine was actually arrested outside the main door of the Peking Friendship Store just for talking with a foreign diplomat.)

Normally, I have avoided the Friendship Stores, but when I arrived in Canton a rather Westernized Chinese friend asked me if I would accompany him there to buy a large three-hundred-yuan radio–cassette player, or ghetto blaster, currently the rage in China. My friend, who was dressed for the occasion in a Western suit, necktie, and trenchcoat, and who spoke English and longed passionately to go to the United States, had somehow managed to acquire the necessary foreign-currency script needed for his purchase. He asked me to come along as a foreign front man, since local Chinese are still theoretically not allowed to shop at these stores or even to hold foreign currency. When we arrived we found, not the gloomy place I had remembered, but a new, modern building situated next to a recently opened fast-food outlet called the Friendship Cafe, whose plastic and stainless steel accouterments glittered as brightly as those in any Wendy's or Kentucky Fried Chicken. A steady stream of people was pouring out of the entrance of the Friendship Store itself, lugging mattresses, television sets, washing machines, radio–cassette players, clothes, cosmetics, and bags full of imported groceries. Many of the people were clearly local Chinese like my friend.

"Can Chinese now buy things at Friendship Stores?" I asked incredulously.

"They're not supposed to, but they do it anyway," he replied, a naughty grin breaking out across his face. "If you dress up like an overseas Chinese and have foreign-currency script, the clerks usually don't say anything. They want to sell as much as they can, because they can get bonuses. It's the responsibility system in action. Business is business." This was not the last time I would hear this particular adage in Canton.

Stepping inside the front door, I was astonished at how similar the atmosphere was to that of a Western department store. The centrally heated and air-conditioned interior was well lit, and the glass counters were filled with tastefully displayed merchandise. Each department was marked by a digital electronic sign. Thousands of shoppers, including some in tailored Mao jackets and squat caps—obviously Party cadres—were hunched over counters inspecting the store's wares. Occasionally, an overworked clerk would snap at a persistent customer, but most of the staff appeared helpful and polite. They went about the task of selling with a concentration I had never previously observed in a large state-run Chinese store. At the foot of a staircase leading to the second floor, I spotted something that helped explain this new attitude, a posted announcement written in battered English from the store's employees to its customers:

YOU ARE WELCOME TO ELECT FINE SHOP ASSISTANTS

Dear Guests: Our store is performing a service competition on fair trade. Best service and courtesy and convenience to our guests. We honestly invite guests to give us valuable suggestions and to elect fine shop assistants who make you satisfactory according to the following:

1. Greet guest warmly and initiatively. Say "three words" (Greeting response to guests, questions, and farewell) well to guests, speak gently, behave politely toward guests.

2. Introduce guests articles in detail. Help guest chose articles. Make everything convent to guests.

3. Skillfull business, accurate change and article packing in a quick, proper and firm manner.

4. Keep neat and clean looks. Manage counters well. Don't delay guests because of private affairs.

Guangzhou Friendship Store

In the old days, a store's management and staff took a devil-may-care attitude toward its customers. If customers became fed up with poor management and sloppy service, so much the better. They would shop elsewhere and make less work for the offending clerks. But the truth was that there was no "elsewhere." Chinese consumers were prisoners. They had to shop *someplace*, and every store was run by the state. Employees had no incentive to sell anything, since their wages remained constant regardless of their performance. But with the advent of the responsibility system, which prescribed that people should be paid according to their work, and with businesses becoming increasingly competitive, stores began scrambling to increase their sales by upgrading service. As a result, solicitious signs addressed to consumers such as the one in the Friendship Store began to appear in both English and Chinese; and if the English was often clumsy, it still suggested the degree to which a new spirit of individual initiative and of competition had become a part of doing business in China.

At the Friendship Store, my friend was waited on by an efficient young woman who patiently took several radio-cassette players out of their boxes to show him, even though nine or ten other customers were crowding around the counter. My presence there as a foreigner was completely unnecessary. So accustomed were the clerks to selling to anyone with foreign-currency script that they did not even challenge my friend to see if he was a local in disguise. As we left the store, my friend held the cassette player with obvious satisfaction. He had a triumphant smile on his face, a Marlboro clamped between his teeth; the tails of his trenchcoat snapped behind him. Looking at him, I was again struck by how quickly the archetypal model of youth, at least in urban China, had changed. My friend was not a proletarian hero who aspired to serve workers, peasants, and soldiers in the countryside. Although he was still a patriotic Chinese citizen, he had other aspirations. He wanted to become educated, to go abroad, to find excitement and a materially better life. He was the embodiment of a new, privileged, Westernized, coastal intelligentsia that was once again growing up in China's cities as contacts with the outside world increased.

China had last given rise to such a class of young people in the nineteen-twenties and nineteen-thirties. So Westernized had many of them become—having been educated or having lived abroad, experiences once again becoming extremely common for young Chinese—that they ended up feeling closer to the cosmopolitan urban worlds of Shanghai, Canton, Paris, London, New York, and San Francisco than to the vast rural hinterland of China, where 80 per cent of their fellow countrymen lived. Do Chinese leaders today still remember, as cities like Canton once again become Westernized hubs of commerce, that it was precisely such divisions between cities and the countryside which Mao's revolution had set out to erase?

Two things have transformed Canton into one of China's most cosmopolitan cities over the past few years: its closeness, as mentioned, to Hong Kong and Macao, and the boom in foreign petroleum exploration in the South China Sea, which is estimated to contain between 30 billion and 100 billion barrels of crude oil, the equivalent of the North Sea fields. In 1978, when policy reversals made at the Third Plenum of the Eleventh Party Congress began precipitating changes in almost every aspect of Chinese life, the Chinese oil industry, which after the Russian departure in 1959 had struggled to develop through "self-reliance," turned about-face to the West for capital and technology. In April, 1979, the Chinese signed contracts with forty-eight different oil companies from thirteen separate countries to make geophysical surveys in a 350,000-square-kilometer area in the South China Sea, resulting in the discovery of 315 oil-bearing geological structures. When the first round of bidding for actual drilling rights came up in 1982, the China National Offshore Oil Corporation, the government agency responsible for oil exploration and drilling in China, set up two subsidiary companies to take charge of the operations, the China Nanhai East Oil Corporation in Canton, and the China Nanhai West Oil Corporation located in Zhanjiang, a once-sleepy town south of Canton which was a French concession from 1898 to 1943.

If estimates prove to be even close to accurate, these reaches of the South China coast, between Canton and Zhanjiang, by 1990 could become the center of a foreign capital investment boom that could easily reach $20 billion. Already, the *South China Morning Post* in Hong Kong has dubbed Canton "China's Houston." Naturally enough, China is banking on the future export earnings of this oil to modernize other sectors of its economy. *Washington Post* correspondent Michael Weisskopf estimates that if oil revenues reached $16 billion by 1990—a conservative estimate—they could pay for 23 per cent of the nation's projected imports. China has much riding on offshore oil; and it is the dizzying anticipation of this new source of hard currency that has helped propel China's Communist government into a rapid dependence on Western oil companies. Nonetheless, the risk-contract formulas, where the foreign oil companies initially bear all exploration costs and will "profit share" once oil is flowing and expenses are paid back, are not bad deals for the Chinese.

The French-owned company TOTAL began explorations in 1980 and was joined by the United States–owned Atlantic Richfield Corporation in 1982. By the middle of 1984, China had signed seventeen contracts with twenty-eight major international foreign petroleum companies. American firms alone had committed over $600 million. Most of these companies set up headquarters in Canton, where many foreign personnel found themselves both living and working in hotels and feeling lucky to have found the space. British Petroleum and Exxon rented whole floors at the new White Swan Hotel, taking up one-third of the hotel's capacity. This thirty-four-story first-class hotel advertises itself as a "luxury business resort" and is built on Shamian Island in the Pearl River, which has had a long history of being residentially occupied by foreigners. In 1859, it became an exclusive foreign concession controlled by the French and British, who posted guards at the bridge to keep out unauthorized Chinese: a situation that remained the norm until the nineteen-forties.

Other foreign businessmen took up residence at the Dongfang (Oriental) Hotel, where the general manager, Yang Xiangting, noted apologetically, "Although we don't have enough guest rooms, we'll do our best to receive our oil-cooperative partners, [and] do everything we can to make sure they feel at home." But foreign businessmen in China have gotten more demanding. Once, they were willing to accept almost any accommodation simply for the privilege of being allowed into China to negotiate. Now, with the thrill of just being there beginning to wear off, businessmen are demanding the conveniences of life back home. In turn, Chinese leaders have quickly realized that such facilities are a prerequisite for doing business with Western firms and have started trying to make up for lost time.

The Chinese-owned Nanhai West Oil Corporation has, for instance, set up a hotel and residential complex near the port of Zhanjiang with apartments and villas built in what the *Beijing Review* called "French Provincial style," as well as shops, a club, a swimming pool, and tennis courts on the premises. The China Nanhai Oil Joint Service Corporation also has plans to construct a thirty-eight-story building, to be called the South China Sea Oil Center, in Canton (with funds from six foreign banks) to accommodate offices of the new foreign arrivals. Of all the new construction being undertaken in Guangdong, however, nothing quite equals the China Hotel, which had a "soft," or partial, opening in December, 1983, and a "grand" opening in June, 1984. This nineteen-story, 1,200-room, $100 million white-and-gold colossus towers over its surroundings like the Potala over Lhasa. Like the Great Wall and Jianguo hotels in Peking, the China Hotel is a joint venture, in this case between China's Yangcheng Service Development Corporation and the Shin Ho Ch'eng Development Ltd., an investment consortium from Hong Kong, and like the two hotels in Peking, it has foreign management. A contract signed with Hong Kong's New World Hotels International provides for management, including a staff of twelve foreigners in key positions and one hundred Hong Kong Chinese working under a German general manager.

Like the Great Wall Hotel, the China Hotel offers features to guests which have hitherto been unknown in China: an indoor gym, a sauna, massage facilities, tennis courts, a swimming pool, a beauty salon, a ballroom with Dolby sound, eighteen food and beverage outlets, a nine-lane bowling alley, a fleet of Mercedes-Benzes, a 400-car underground parking garage, a shopping arcade, and an office tower and residential wing with 250 deluxe furnished apartments, most of which had been rented by foreign oil companies before they were even completed.

When I arrived at the China Hotel for an overnight visit, I found a lobby of gleaming red granite in which hung two enormous, glittering crystal chandeliers that looked like upside-down Mayan temples. Lounging languorously on a couch under one of the chandeliers was an officer from the People's Liberation Army. Several Chinese children were running and sliding along the polished floors as if they were ice skaters. A phalanx of Chinese obviously from the countryside and led by a paunchy overseas Chinese in a Western-style leisure suit, his hair coiffed and combed with a liberal dab of Brylcreem, came through the lobby, looking thunderstruck by the opulence.

Here in Canton, where so many Chinese come from abroad to regale their relatives left at home, it is not possible, as it is in Peking, to keep such a hotel as a privileged foreign preserve. In fact, all day long I saw awed Chinese families being led through the lobby to one of the hotel's restaurants by overseas relatives. It was practically the first time I had been in a hotel or restaurant in China where foreigners and Chinese could eat and mix together without triggering inquiries from security guards.

Everywhere in the China Hotel were myriad Western touches: the bathrooms stocked with bars of Imperial Leather soap made in England by Cussons and packages of shampoo made by Kamil in West Germany; the English-language *South China Morning Post* from Hong Kong slipped under the door each A.M.; the telephones, American touch-tone style; the color televisions made in Japan; the heating and cooling controls made by Honeywell in the United States. When I stopped at the Corner Bar, one of four hotel lounges, I was greeted at the door by a solicitous and neatly groomed Chinese in a dark Western-style suit and checkered necktie. "Good evening, sir. Would you care for a cocktail before dinner?" he asked in excellent English.

As he squired me to a stool at the bar, I noticed from the tag on his lapel that he had taken the European given name Charles. "Do not hesitate to call me if there is anything further I can do for you," Charles Chen said graciously, handing me a drink menu as I sat down. At the end of the bar I noticed a brand-new Italian espresso machine, and was just thinking how quaint and archaic the small coffee shop in Taicheng suddenly seemed, when my reveries were broken by a bartender whose name tag identified him as Wister Chu. He was dressed in a black bow tie, white shirt, red vest and cummerbund, and black trousers. Approaching from behind the bar, he asked in wooden English, "What would you like to drink, please, sir?"

Wondering what sort of "expertise" this Western bar actually had, I asked for a Tequila Sunrise. No effort had been made here to Sinify the drinks in the manner of the Chinese Peace Hotel—formerly the Cathay Hotel—in Shanghai, where the bar offered a Peace Cocktail, a Friendship Cocktail, a Panda Cocktail, and the *pièce de résistance*, the Million-Dollar Cocktail.

"Very well, sir," said Wister Chu, and set to work. While I waited for my Tequila Sunrise, I noted that all the bartenders and waitresses wore tags with European names. Besides Wister and Charles there were Pierre, Felix, Winnie, and Angela. In many Chinese cities, young upward-mobile youths with some familiarity with a foreign language are taking European Christian names. During the Cultural Revolution such a practice would, of course, have been utterly inconceivable, tantamount to "taking the capitalist road"; but in 1984 such names carried no counter-revolutionary odium. Far from being a political liability, they seemed to be an asset, conveying as they did a sense of being modern and cosmopolitan.

As I received my Tequila Sunrise, which tasted quite

good, Charles Chen walked over. I asked him how he and his staff had mastered the intricacies of making Western drinks.

"People came up from Hong Kong to teach us," he replied with a pleased smile. "We have a sister hotel there, the New World. To keep our hotel here first-rate, we have had to ask for some help and training from them. In fact, that is where our boss comes from."

"Do any members of your Chinese staff resent having to work under foreign managers?" I asked, still trying to adjust to Chen's use of the word "boss," a term I had never heard in China except to refer to such unacceptable categories of people as "capitalist bosses" or "Soviet bosses."

"No. Why should they?" replied Chen, with a surprised look on his face. "They are good managers, and we are learning from them. Besides, if we had a Chinese hotel manager, we would have more trouble restricting local people from just coming in and wandering around as they please. So, we hired a foreign general manager to carry out our hotel's policy."

It was amazing to hear a Chinese speak of "restricting local people," not because it was an unusual practice, but because few official Chinese ever discuss the subject with foreigners so unselfconsciously. Chen, however, acknowledged it without any suggestion of hesitation or circumspection, as if it was the most natural thing in the world for a Chinese hotelier—who was working in a country that was at least theoretically "under the dictatorship of the proletariat"—to want to keep his countrymen out of his hotel lest they scuff up the rugs and wear out the furniture. The fact that Chen felt no evident uneasiness with this whole concept suggested the degree to which local employees in these new hothouse areas of foreign comfort and convenience may have internalized the values of their clients. In fact, they may have internalized them so effectively that foreigners will no longer have to do anything to protect their own glorious isolation as they had to do in times past.

"Well, actually, we don't keep everyone out," continued Chen upon reflection. "But we just can't allow anyone to come in and sit in the air-conditioned lobby all day. We want to be a local hotel, but for people who can afford it. Of course, many overseas Chinese stay here and like to invite their relatives to come and eat. That's fine, and we can't object to it."

Charles Chen earned 180 yuan a month, almost four times what an average factory worker makes. Rank-and-file staff members make 130 yuan a month. Everyone was looking forward to bonuses, which were to be calculated after the first six months according to the success of each unit in providing service to hotel guests. The responsibility system was alive and well at the China Hotel.

"And how is the staff succeeding in providing first-class service at the China Hotel?" I asked Chen.

"We are learning," he replied confidently. "We have not had much experience yet, so sometimes things might not be quite right. For instance, maybe a staff member makes a mistake, maybe one of them will come to work in the winter with green long underwear sticking out of his or her uniform. When we see these things, even though the staff member may be a little embarrassed, we must criticize them."

The word "criticize" (*piping*) rang in my ears. Not so long ago the word had quite a different connotation in China. To "criticize" someone meant to level charges of erroneous ideological thought at that person, an allegation that potentially carried the most dire consequences. Thinking about China before the open-door policy made me wonder about Charles Chen's own past.

"As a young man, I joined the People's Liberation Army," he told me. "After I got out of the Army, I attended the Canton Foreign Languages Institute. When I graduated from there, I was assigned to work as a cadre in the Canton railroad station."

"Are you a member of the Chinese Communist Party?" I asked on hearing the word "cadre."

"Yes," answered Chen, stiffening a little, like a soldier who suddenly finds himself being inspected. "I became a Party member in 1973."

As I sat digesting the idea of a maître d' in a Western-style cocktail lounge being not only a member of the Chinese Communist Party but a former member of the People's Liberation Army, Wister Chu took an order for a Margarita from an American sitting on the next stool. Turning on a United States–made blender full blast, he mixed the drink. Then, showing only the slightest hesitation, he rimmed the glass with salt and set it on the bar with a bowl of peanuts. In his stiff English, he said, "Please try some. They are roasted by our own German chef."

"Have you ever been abroad?" I asked, turning back to Chen.

"Yes. I have been to Hong Kong to receive some training with a delegation of waiters and policemen," he replied with a smile.

"What kind of impression did Hong Kong make on you?"

"Oh, very nice," replied Chen, his face breaking out into a full-fledged grin. "We went to discos and enjoyed ourselves very much."

"Would you like to go back?"

"Yes, of course. We Chinese like to go to Hong Kong because life is good there . . . better than here. Everybody likes to go where life is good. Everyone likes to have fun."

The notion of "having fun" has only recently attained even a partial acceptability in China. Under Mao, all Chinese were supposed to dedicate themselves heart and soul to the task of building revolutionary socialism. Pleasure-seeking was considered a frivolous and dangerous waste of time. Indeed, all music, art, literature, and other forms of "entertainment" were geared to advancing the political line of the Chinese Communist Party. But now Charles Chen was telling me openly that "everybody likes to have fun," almost as if nonpolitical fun were an inalienable right. All across China I found young people dedicating themselves to the notion of fun, expressed in Chinese by the elusive phrase *renao*, which literally means "heat and noise." (Young Chinese, for instance, speak of "going out to look for heat and noise": *qu kan renao*.) And as more and more leisure-time activities like reading love stories or science fiction, playing pool, watching foreign films and television (in July, 1984, China Central Television bought sixty-four hours of programming from CBS), hanging out at restaurants and coffee shops, and even indulging in courtship have become permissible, the notion of "having fun" has had a rebirth.

In Taishan county, for instance, the local labor-union organization even sponsors weekly Saturday-night dances for young people. A few days after my conversation with Charles Chen, I attended one such dance with a European friend. After paying .30 yuan to a gatekeeper at the union compound—which was situated across from a main movie theater and pool hall, one of Taicheng's main hang-out spots for idle youth—we climbed a set of stairs to a meeting room from which we could hear the distant strains of "Swanee River" drifting out into the night. Arriving at the doorway, we peered into the "dance hall," which was completely dark except for the illumination cast by several strings of Christmas-tree lights hung around the walls of the otherwise bare room. As my eyes adjusted to the dim light, I saw that while there were many youths in the room, only three or four couples were actually dancing; and in spite of the seductive darkness, these couples were made up, not of youths of the opposite sex taking the opportunity for some modest physical contact, but of boys dancing with boys and girls with girls. Moreover, as we watched, it became obvious that the state of the dancing art here in Taishan was rather low. The couples moved around the room to the music in jerking motions, as if following diagrams on the floor.

We had hardly been in this curious dance hall for more than five minutes when a young woman timidly approached. Hearing me speak Chinese to a young swain (wearing tight jeans and a plaid jacket), she stepped forward and asked me if I would teach her how to dance. Amazed at her boldness, feeling somewhat like a modern-day missionary asked to preach a sermon on a new gospel to the Chinese masses, I stepped out onto the floor and began to lead her in the box step. As we chatted, she told me that her name was "Miss Wu," that during the daytime she worked in an electrical wire factory, and that she loved to practice dancing and listen to Western pop music in the evening as a diversion from her boring job. Actually, conversation was difficult to maintain with Miss Wu, not only because the music was loud (we were now dancing to an up-rhythm version of "Home on the Range") but because while we danced she looked almost exclusively at my feet, making it rather hard to discern what she was saying. In fact, every youth in the room was looking at my European friend and me with great intensity, as if they expected us to momentarily unlock the riddle of the universe. No one in the room was going to miss out on one instant of this dance lesson from four imported feet! The open-door policy may have meant the mastering of Western science and technology to China's leaders, but to these Taishan youths craving a little foreign culture and glamour, it meant learning how to dance and having some fun.

However, like most other forms of "fun," or *renao*, in China, dancing clearly had its limits. These limits became self-evident when the tape deck suddenly began to emit the sounds of "When the Saints Go Marching In," and my friend burst into a jitterbug before his amazed and delighted partner. Almost as one, the other youths in the room rose and crowded around him to watch. Just as some of the bolder boys began to laugh and clap, a cadre in a gray Mao suit, whom I had previously noticed sitting beside the tape deck, sprang into action. He jumped to his feet, walked over to the performance, and motioned my friend to cease with a palms-forward fluttering gesture, the kind someone makes trying to dissipate a bad smell.

When he finally stopped, the crestfallen youths surged

around him, begging him to dance with me, explaining that the cadre had only objected because my friend was dancing in such a flamboyant manner with a Chinese girl rather than a foreigner. My embarrassed refusal to become his jitterbug partner for the edification of a dance-hungry crowd of Chinese youths ended this particular instance of *renao*. The youths returned to their chairs, disappointment written all over their faces. The cadre, perhaps hoping to reinvest himself with the mantle of authority among his charges, began to dance with one of the young women himself, but in a fashion so unrhythmical that he looked like a mechanical man.

The quest for fun in China today is not limited to urban youths. Even rural peasants are looking for some *renao*. Last March in Lingbao county, Henan province, peasants held a cross-country motorbike race. A photograph in the *China Daily* showing scores of contestants bolting from the starting line was headlined RACING INTO THE FUTURE. The caption below noted: "With more money and free time under the responsibility system, peasants who once lived by the old adage of 'A hoe in the field and a pillow at home' are now turning to recreational activities."

I asked Charles Chen if he, as a Communist Party member, feared that too much concern with "fun" could lead to spiritual pollution (the campaign was just ending at the time of our conversation). He replied seriously, "I'm not worried. Anyway, here at the hotel, we don't want to pollute anyone. We just want to do business and make friends with people from foreign lands."

Canton, exploding with capitalist energy and bombarded with Western influences, had a way of jolting me each time I turned around. Billboard advertisements were everywhere. The streets were filled with newly opened private restaurants and shops. Private taxis roamed the streets looking for fares. Black-marketeer moneychangers accosted me, apparently fearless of arrest. Beggars slept in doorways.

"If I worry about anything in China today, it is Canton," Peter Gautschi, executive vice-president of the legendary

Peninsula Group in Hong Kong—which in addition to the Jianguo Hotel in Peking was about to open the 1,147-room deluxe Garden Hotel in Canton—told me when I asked him if he had any reservations about the direction China was going. "It has all been moving so fast. I had one meeting with members of the Pearl River Construction Company, which is building the Garden Hotel. One Chinese was smoking Kents and another Marlboros, a third ordered a Heineken, and a fourth a glass of Hennessy cognac. What concerns me is the possibility that things in Canton may get so far ahead of the rest of the country that Peking may blow the whistle on them."

Peking, however, seemed little concerned by all that I was observing. On April 13, 1984, Chen Muhua, State Councilor and Minister of Foreign Economic Relations and Trade, reaffirmed China's commitment to maintaining an open-door policy, saying, moreover, that China would expand its trade with more countries and regions in an effort to quadruple the value of its exports and imports by the year 2000. "To achieve this goal, foreign funds will continue to be used, technology imported, international economic and technical cooperation improved," she proclaimed. "The open-door policy will be implemented unswervingly."

On April 23, 1984, just before Ronald Reagan arrived in Peking, Dr. Armand Hammer, chairman of the Occidental Petroleum Corporation, announced that his company had concluded two-and-one-half years of negotiations with the China National Coal Development Corporation on a $600 million joint venture to develop the Pingshuo open-pit coal mines in China's inland province of Shanxi. The project would be the largest joint venture yet between China and any other foreign corporation or government, and would put American managers in charge of the 14.7-square-mile mining operation (said to contain 1.4 billion tons of coal) for thirteen years. It would also inject a massive amount of capital, technology, and foreign influence into Shanxi, one of China's poorest and most tradition-bound provinces. It would clearly have an impact on Shanxi every bit as profound as that of the foreign oil companies on South China.

When Ronald Reagan arrived in China, in April of 1984, almost his first act was to initial an agreement that could clear the way for the American nuclear power industry to participate in building twelve new nuclear plants in China worth an estimated $20 billion. While in Paris in June of 1984, Premier Zhao Ziyang announced that China and France had concluded an accord designed to make French investment in China easier, and that they were close to an agreement on a contract for the construction of a multi-million-dollar nuclear power plant in Canton. When a French reporter asked him what would ultimately remain of Chinese Communist ideology if China continued to modernize and open up to the West at such a rapid rate, Zhao replied, "I have complete confidence in the ideas of Marx and Lenin. But I deal with the concrete situation in which China finds itself."

Zhao's belief that China's "concrete situation" could somehow be detached from the country's official ideology and dealt with separately without creating a schizophrenic contradiction seemed unrealistic to me. How, I wondered, would China's leaders ever succeed in reconciling the gathering force of Western influence now entering their country through the "open door" with all the old revolutionary notions upon which the Chinese Revolution had been built, and to which the Party, at least officially, still subscribed?

They seemed to imagine that China, like a push-me/pull-you, could maintain a semblance of socialist purity while in actual practice it drifted more and more into the thrall of the Western capitalist world. Perhaps they assumed that each force would counteract the other, creating a balance. But had China's leaders taken into account the real seductive power of the West and all that it represents? Perhaps not, for the forces of Westernization in China during the 1980s clearly seem to be winning the tug of war. In fact, by the middle of 1984 they had gained such momentum that they seemed to have come close to eclipsing the old values of socialist revolution and Mao Zedong Thought entirely.

In 1949, just before the final Communist victory on the China mainland, the well-known leftist writer and critic Mao Dun gave a lecture in which he attacked those Chinese who looked to the West for inspiration. Denouncing such people as having sold out to "compradore culture" (compradores were those Chinese who worked for foreign companies before "liberation"), Mao Dun's talk set the tone for the "rectification movement" the Chinese Communist Party soon began to launch against the contamination of culture by Western bourgeois ideas of all kinds. "Compradore culture, which might be termed the godchild of imperialism, has relied on our big cities as its base camps and has sent out its probing attacks from there," proclaimed Mao Dun. "The petty bourgeoisie is the hothouse soil most conducive to compradore culture, a soil in which it will always take root. The worshipping of Western people, the intoxication with European and American life, the notion that 'the moon shines brighter abroad than here at home'—or, to put it more succinctly, the sowing of the seeds of an inferiority complex in the minds of our people—this is the speciality of compradore culture."

In those early days of the Chinese Revolution, the Party struggled militantly not only against "compradore culture" in the large coastal cities in which it had taken root, but against the whole outside capitalist/imperialist world that threatened not only to dissolve China's cultural identity but to deprive it of its economic and political independence as well. Now the historical wheel appears to have come full circle. Once again China is looking westward. This time, of course, the country is unified and stronger. Moreover, it is inviting its former imperialist adversaries back in, rather than being encroached upon by foreign armies, traders, and evangelists. In these important respects, at least, the chemistry of China's reconnection with the West is different.

But as Westerners flood back into China, reviving foreign

enclaves of privilege in the old coastal cities that once comprised the ignominious "treaty ports," one cannot help but wonder what has become of that very tender place in China's collective psyche which in the past had felt so humiliated in the face of Western wealth, power, and technological superiority. At least in those areas through which I travelled in 1983 and 1984, the Chinese appeared to have at least temporarily lost touch with this current in their recent history. China itself seemed on the verge of passing irrevocably from one historical era into another. Exactly what it was in the process of becoming had not yet been clearly spelled out. For the moment, China's new leaders were simply trying to "modernize" their country. How it was all supposed to look when the process was completed, no one seemed to know or care. But as I left China for home, I could not but wonder whether the changes I had seen in Guangdong were not the unarticulated vision of all China's future.

Orville Schell is a noted China observer who has visited that country many times in recent years. He has written on China (and other subjects) for *The New Yorker, Rolling Stone, The New York Times, Natural History, Asia Magazine,* and many other magazines and newspapers. He is the author of *In the People's Republic, "Watch Out for the Foreign Guests!",* and *Modern China,* and coeditor of *The China Reader, I, II & III.* His most recent non-China book is *Modern Meat.*

DATE DUE